CHRONICLES OF OLD LAS VEGAS

EXPLORING SIN CITY'S HIGH-STAKES HISTORY

Published in the United States by:
Museyon, Inc.
20 E. 46th St., Ste. 1400
New York, NY 10017

Museyon is a registered trademark.
Visit us online at www.museyon.com

ISBN 978-0-9846334-1-8

71901959

Printed in China

12/18

To Jim Scarpace,

who showed me the
best parts of Las Vegas.

CHRONICLES OF OLD LAS VEGAS

CHAPTER 1.

THE SPRING

It started as an oasis.

Picture a grassy meadow surrounded by an inhospitable desert.
For millennia, that was the place we now call Las Vegas. Almost
miraculously, over an expanse nearly 40 miles long and 15 miles wide,
a spring bubbled up through the Mojave Desert floor. Its fresh water
supported plant and animal life, and the indigenous Paiute tribe.

The Paiute believed the earth to be sacred. Though they had no private
property rights, they were protective of their spring; it was Paiute
ancestral land for as many as 4,000 years. When the white man's culture
eventually encroached, it was Chief Tecopa, the final leader entrusted
to protect the spring, who gave up the indigenous people's sacred
oasis peacefully.

The Paiute didn't know that, for 300 years starting in 1521, Europeans
had called their grassy meadow New Spain. And in 1776, when
missionaries blazed a path between New Mexico and California called
the Old Spanish Trail, the Paiute had no idea.

← Captian John, a Paiute Indian, circa 1903

These indigenous people were nomads who spoke a language similar to the ancient Aztecs. In winter, they wore coats made from rabbit pelts, and when the weather got hot, the Paiute went nearly naked. Five to 10 families would roam together as a group, perhaps as many as 100 people. In the winter, all tribes-members would gather in one or two semi-permanent settlements. Then in the spring, they would scatter again in their nomadic quests for food and adventure.

Meanwhile, merchants and missionaries crisscrossed the territory along the L-shaped Old Spanish Trail. It was the easiest but not the most direct route to Los Angeles; some explorers continued to search for a shorter way. In November 1829, a team of 60 Spanish merchants led by the explorer and trader Antonio Armijo strayed from the trail. Their scout, Rafael Rivera, discovered the verdant oasis that he proclaimed "Las Vegas," "the meadows" in Spanish. Armijo's traders were the first Europeans to behold the unexpected oasis.

In 1844, John C. Frémont, adventurer and son-in-law of a prominent U.S. Senator, surveyed the Nevada Territory with Kit Carson as his guide. During a five-month journey with 25 men, Frémont's cartographers mapped the spring's territory in detail. Frémont wrote: "Two narrow streams of water, four or five feet deep, gush suddenly, with a quick current, from two singularly large springs…the taste of the water is good but rather too warm to be agreeable."

The Paiute attacked the intruders. Chief Tecopa and his warriors attempted to chase Carson and Frémont away from the spring, grossly underestimating the foe they had encountered. A three-day skirmish ensued; Carson subdued the Paiute with the crack of his pistol, a sound heard at the spring for the first time. Tecopa soon reversed himself, serving as a crucial intermediary between two cultures. However, following this first encounter, Frémont cast a harsh eye on the indigenous hunter-gatherers, writing that the Paiute he observed were "humanity in its lowest form and most elementary state."

An undated photograph of Della Fisk and Chief Tecopa, Pahrump Valley, Nevada

Despite the altercation with the Paiute, when Congress published Frémont's report, settlers had one more reason to head west. And, when President Lincoln proclaimed Nevada as America's 36th state on October 31, 1864, a metamorphosis at the Las Vegas springs was inevitable. Tecopa realized that the Paiute must adapt or die.

With the arrival of white settlers, the indigenous people were soon embroiled in conflicts over land ownership and the produce from fields that were irrigated by the spring. Chief Tecopa, just two years younger than Frémont, represented the final generation of nomads.

TODAY'S PAIUTE

In July 1970, the U.S. government recognized the Paiute Tribe as a Sovereign Nation.

In 1983, an act of Congress restored an additional 3,850 acres of land to the Paiute Tribe. Now known as the Snow Mountain Reservation, it is located about 25 miles from today's Las Vegas Strip.

The Paiute have created three modern golf courses on the Reservation, open to the public year-round.

For more information, contact:
Las Vegas Paiute Golf Resort
10325 Nu-Wav Kaiv Boulevard
Las Vegas, Nevada 89124
800-711-2833 or 702-658-1400

Each spring, the Paiute open the Snow Mountain Reservation to the public on Memorial Day weekend, rain or shine, to host their popular Pow-Wow. The Paiute people sing and dance their ancient tribal customs, to keep that culture alive for younger generations.

For more information, contact:
lvpaiutetribe.com/powwow
702-383-1515

Near downtown Las Vegas, the Paiute own and operate a cigar store, the largest humidor in Nevada:
Tribal Smoke Shop
1225 N. Main Street
Las Vegas, NV 89101
702-366-1101
lvpaiutesmokeshop.com

Paiute Indian group posed in front of adobe house, circa 1909-1932

Though his name meant "Wildcat," Tecopa kept it peaceful. He
displayed his willingness to accommodate the white settlers by wearing
his best European attire and was frequently seen in a silk top hat and a
red marching-band jacket with gold braid. Elsewhere in America, native
people were being herded off the land and slaughtered along the Trail of
Tears, but not so at the springs in Tecopa's Las Vegas. He encouraged
a bloodless assimilation for the Paiute, leading them to work for wages
in white culture, as laborers in the mines and as domestic helpers on
the ranches. Ten percent of the Paiute population died of typhoid or
other European diseases to which they had no immunity. Many others
suffered psychological shock, witnesses to the end of nomadic life in
North America.

One of the first settlers to own a piece of the meadow was Octavius
Decatur Gass from Ohio, who eventually expanded his holdings to 640
acres. He hired Paiute workers to harvest his wheat, oats and barley.
After the first harvest, they planted fruits and vegetables too. Other

THE SPRINGS TODAY

In 1978, the spring at Las Vegas was added to the National Register of Historic Places, and designated as a Nevada landmark as well.

A visit to the Springs Preserve can be a welcome respite from the bustle of the Las Vegas Strip. Open seven days a week, from 10 a.m. to 6 p.m.

Springs Preserve
333 South Valley View Boulevard
Las Vegas, NV 89107
702-822-7700
springspreserve.org

Col. JOHN C. FREMONT,
REPUBLICAN CANDIDATE FOR PRESIDENT OF THE UNITED STATES.

Colonel John C. Frémont, 1856

landowners followed. The transfer of the oasis was complete; pioneers mixed with native people to create the first permanent settlement in the valley.

Tecopa lived to see his people into the 20th century; he died in 1904, buried with his son and grandson at the Chief Tecopa Cemetery in Pahrump Valley, Nevada. In 1971, Nevada Governor Mike O'Callaghan dedicated a state memorial to the Chief at his gravesite.

Meanwhile, Frémont became the new Republican Party's first candidate for U.S. President. (He lost to one-term Democrat James Buchanan.) He later became the Governor of the Arizona Territory. Today, counties in four states, and the central boulevard in downtown Las Vegas, are named for him.

Helen J. Stewart, the wife of a prominent rancher, inherited the land and water rights once owned by O. D. Gass. She deeded part of that property to create the Las Vegas Indian Colony for her Paiute friends.

In 1978, the Las Vegas spring was added to the National Register of Historic Places. The Springs Preserve, located about four miles from the Strip (and open to the public, seven days a week), is the meadow's last 180 undeveloped acres, where fresh water breaks through the Mojave Desert floor. Las Vegas remains an oasis.

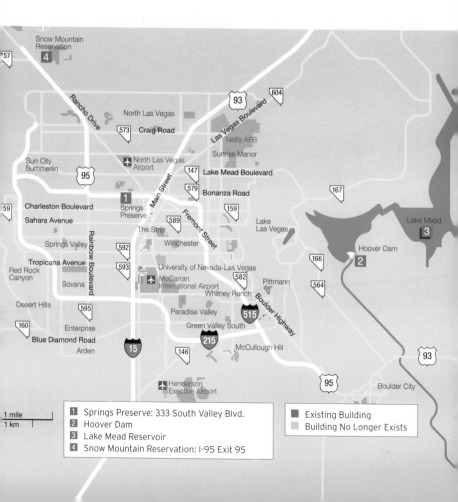

1 mile
1 km

1 Springs Preserve: 333 South Valley Blvd.
2 Hoover Dam
3 Lake Mead Reservoir
4 Snow Mountain Reservation: I-95 Exit 95

■ Existing Building
■ Building No Longer Exists

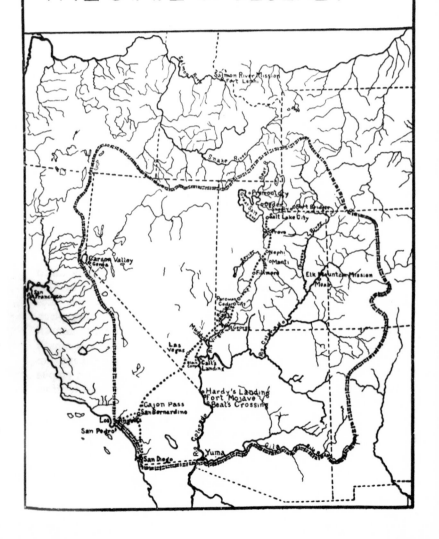

CHAPTER 2.

NATIVE AMERICANS VS. LATTER-DAY SAINTS

Nevada's indigenous people, the Paiute, couldn't imagine the developments that would happen on their land in the 19th century. It started with a group of white militiamen who came in the name of the Church of Jesus Christ of Latter Day Saints.

The church was founded in Fayette, New York, in 1830, with young Joseph Smith as its spiritual leader. In 1820, at just 14 years old, Smith claimed that God and Jesus Christ appeared before him as visions in the woods. In 1823, Smith was visited again, this time by an angel named Moroni who anointed him as a prophet; in honor of the angel, Smith called his followers Mormons. According to Mormon beliefs, four years later, Moroni revealed to Smith a set of golden plates, buried in a hillside. Smith translated the inscriptions on the plates in 1829 and named his translation the Book of Mormon. By 1830, when Smith claimed that the Lord instructed him to proselytize to other faiths, the local Christians had heard enough. The Latter-Day Saints were driven out of New York.

← Map of the proposed Mormon State of Deseret

The death of Joseph and Hiram Smith in Carthage jail, June 27th, 1844.
Lithograph by Charles G. Crehen, 1851

Seeking relative safety in Ohio's Western Reserve and in Jackson
County, Missouri, the Mormons added converts, but still found no
welcome. Smith was tarred and feathered by a mob in 1832. The
Mormons were prevented from voting in Ohio, then expelled altogether
in 1837. In 1838, the governor of Missouri issued an "Extermination
Order," forcing all Mormons to leave Missouri or be killed. Dozens of
Mormons were massacred or burned out of their homes. That's when the
dynamic Brigham Young stepped up to join Joseph Smith in leading the
Mormon followers to safety in Illinois.

Nauvoo, the town they founded in Illinois, grew rapidly, soon becoming
one of Illinois's largest cities. It was here that Joseph Smith published
many of the doctrines that define the Mormon religion, including its

controversial endorsement of polygamy. In 1844, a riot ensued when Mormons destroyed a printing press where anti-Mormon literature was published. Joseph Smith and his brother were murdered in jail, and the mob scene escalated into a full-scale battle: the Battle of Nauvoo. The Mormons were forcibly driven from the town they'd built.

Brigham Young, now the Mormon president and prophet, realized that his people would be better off in territory outside the U.S. borders (there were 27 states on the North American continent in 1845). From their temporary headquarters in Nebraska, they planned for a vast new home in the Mexican Territory, a dubious choice since America went to battle against Mexico over that land mere months later.

When President Polk called for volunteers in the Mexican-American War, Brigham Young sent the Mormon Battalion. They didn't fight, but like their contemporary John C. Frémont, they explored and mapped the vast territory occupied by the Paiutes that would soon belong to the United States. With the Mexican-American War still raging, the Mormon pioneers crossed the Great Plains, led by Young. They arrived at the Great Salt Lake in July 1847.

When the war ended, the Mexican Cession was annexed to the United States. Would the Mormons again be forced from U.S. territory? Incoming President Millard Fillmore recognized the need for settlers in the new land. He acknowledged all Mormons by appointing Brigham Young as the territorial governor.

The new governor went to work. To President Zachary Taylor, he proposed the State of Deseret, a vast new Mormon state that would stretch from the Oregon Territory to Mexico, including all the Gold Rush territory that was attracting prospectors to the area. Surveying the maps prepared by Frémont and the Mormon Militia, Brigham Young suddenly discovered what the indigenous Paiute Indians had known for millennia: there's water in Las Vegas.

To Young, Las Vegas was a strategic location, a midpoint between Salt Lake City and Los Angeles. On May 10, 1855, he assigned 30 Mormon militiamen to Las Vegas. They were charged as missionaries to convert the Paiute population and take control of the spring and the land surrounding it. The militiamen selected a site along the creek that flowed from the Las Vegas springs, then built a fort of adobe bricks 14 feet high to protect them from the Indians. The Mormon fort was the first building ever to be constructed in Las Vegas.

Own the land? How could anyone own something sacred? Property rights were a foreign concept to the Paiute, who believed that *puha* — spiritual power — inhabited the entire natural world. With little conflict, Mormon soldiers seized the Paiutes' land, then expanded the fort by planting crops in the tribal areas.

Their aggression in Las Vegas didn't last long, because the militiamen were suddenly called back to Utah. In May 1857, Utah's Mormon Militia attempted to prevent the U.S. Army from entering the Salt Lake Valley. The Utah War ensued with a series of skirmishes that continued until July 1858, as the Mormon militia held off the Army. It ended badly, with about 150 people, mostly civilians, dead. Though President James Buchanan eventually granted a full pardon to the Mormon people, Brigham Young was stripped of his governorship, with a non-Mormon installed as his replacement. It was one of America's first conflicts over the separation between church and state: President Buchanan refused to permit Utah's "theodemocracy," a government run by religious leaders. The Mormons' grandiose dreams for a State of Deseret vanished.

That concern over a theodemocracy applied to Las Vegas too, when the U.S. Army discovered the few remaining Mormon settlers at the Las Vegas fort. In a rare twist of racial relations to which history buffs marvel "only in Las Vegas," the United States government enforced an existing treaty that forbade the purchase of Las Vegas land by white settlers. The Mormons, all of them white, were occupying Las Vegas illegally. The ruling was clear: Tribal rights for the Paiute Indians were to be restored and respected. American authorities declared the Mormons' land seizure to be invalid.

The Mormons expressed their displeasure by harassing the Paiute off the land the Mormons considered theirs. This time, the Paiute retaliated, seizing the harvest the Mormons had gathered, claiming it for the indigenous people. Outnumbered, and now without food, the Mormon settlers escaped with their lives, retreating back to the Great Salt Lake.

The Paiute had no use for the Mormon fort, though they left the encroachment standing. Their story would change in 1864 when Nevada became America's 36th state, but for a little while longer, only the native people drank from the spring at Las Vegas.

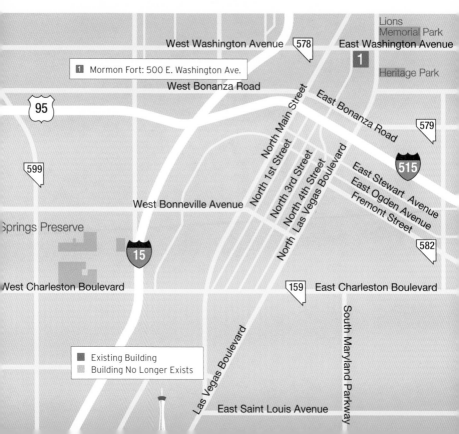

Design for a Union Station

CHAPTER 3.

THE RAILROAD TOWN

Before 1900, when Nevada was a state but there was no town called Las Vegas, Helen J. Stewart, the local postmaster, owned the spring and hundreds of acres surrounding it on the site of the future city.

She inherited the spring and its water rights while pregnant with her fifth child, after her husband was shot to death in 1884. Over the years, she proved to be a shrewd businesswoman, buying additional property to assemble an enormous ranch. At age 36 in 1890, she was the largest landowner in the county.

By 1902, with her children grown, Helen J. Stewart was ready for a change.

Years earlier, the Transcontinental Railroad had been completed in nearby Utah. Now industrialists like Andrew Carnegie and Cornelius Vanderbilt were constructing railroads across America, linking cities and establishing trade routes. First New York and Chicago were linked to

← Caricature of railroad magnate Edward H. Harriman, 1907

HELEN J. STEWART

After Helen J. Stewart sold her ranch and the water rights, she immediately bought 940 acres adjacent to the railroad tracks that generated income for the rest of her life. She presided as the doyen of community affairs, regaled as "The First Lady of Las Vegas."

In 1915, Stewart was the first woman elected to the Clark County School Board, and in 1916 she was one of the first women to sit on a jury. A founder of Christ Episcopal Church, and an authority on the history of southern Nevada, she organized a branch of the Nevada Historical Society in Las Vegas and then became a popular speaker across the state.

Living for so many years on her isolated ranch, Mrs. Stewart developed friendships with many Paiute women. She heard the stories of their lives, then learned how those anecdotes were woven into baskets made by these Native American women. Many Paiute women gave their baskets to Helen; her famed collection swelled to over 550 baskets.

In 1914, Helen's son Will named his baby daughter Helen J. Stewart before learning that the child was mentally disabled. His mother doted on her mentally challenged granddaughter. In her biography of Helen Stewart, published in the Nevada Historical Society Quarterly, Carrie Miller Townley writes, "The doting grandmother had a special love for this exceptional granddaughter, and took great pleasure in each small, slow step forward the child took."

In today's Clark County School District, the elementary school for children with special needs is called The Helen J. Stewart School. It's named for the granddaughter, not her famous grandmother.

All businesses closed on the day of Helen's funeral in 1926. Condolences arrived from across the West, paying tribute to this trailblazing pioneer woman. In downtown Las Vegas, Stewart Avenue is the main thoroughfare parallel to Fremont Street, named in her honor.

San Francisco, then San Francisco was linked to Salt Lake City, the largest community between the Rockies and Los Angeles. Next, it seemed logical to expand the rail service to the south, where Los Angeles meets the ocean.

There was one major problem with this vision: steam engines need water, and fresh produce needs ice. To cross the arid route from Salt Lake City, a railroad would need a depot in the desert.

Edward H. Harriman, owner of the Union Pacific Railroad, and William A. Clark, the former U.S. Senator from Montana, saw the potential. Though they started as competitors, they were soon united by the vision of one railroad. They both called upon Mrs. Stewart.

Stewart sold 1,800 acres, including the Las Vegas water rights, to Clark's railroad enterprise for $55,000 (that's over $1.4 million in today's dollars). Harriman and Clark went to work on their ambitious new project: the San Pedro-Los Angeles and Salt Lake Railroad, connecting the port of Los Angeles at San Pedro, California, to the railroad hub at Salt Lake City, with a major stop in downtown Los Angeles and a visit to the depot near the spring at Las Vegas.

Before the property could be conveyed to the railroad industrialists, a surveyor, J.T. McWilliams, was hired to map the enormous property. In his research, he discovered that an 80-acre parcel of land nearby was still owned by the U.S. government. With his inside information about the railroad's imminent arrival at the Stewart ranch, McWilliams promptly purchased those 80 acres, planning to get rich due to the land's proximity to the railroad tracks. As soon as the new railroad began construction, McWilliams sold small parcels of his townsite for $200 each. (today, it's the area surrounding West Bonanza Road.)

Sales were brisk, but this was rugged territory. With no rail service to provide building materials, the new owners erected tents and ramshackle buildings made of canvas. The McWilliams Townsite soon earned its name as "Ragtown."

By the summer of 1904, when the railroad's construction crew reached Mrs. Stewart's ranch, newspapers gushed, exaggerating the area's virtues. A columnist in the *Los Angeles Daily Times* described the Mojave Desert as "a territory of fabulous richness." Another town of tents sprang up, this time on the railroad property itself. Optimistic laborers of all sorts awaited the opportunities that a rail line would bring.

To handle the crowd, Charles "Pop" Squires erected the 30-room Hotel Las Vegas: a huge canvas structure 140 feet long and 40 feet wide, with additional tents for a dining room and kitchen. Until the following winter, this massive tent served as the center of all social activities.

A depot in the desert was an alluring responsibility for former Senator Clark. The San Pedro-Los Angeles and Salt Lake Railroad owned everything, from the water to the dirt. Clark got to construct an entire town, one that would be of service to his company. All building materials would be transported to Las Vegas by rail, and all tenants in the depot would pay him rent. The town's future residents would buy land from the railroad and then pay for its water. That spring water would also serve the railroad's freight customers. Midway on the route, the Las Vegas depot was the place to ice down produce from California and feed livestock headed for slaughter.

Fremont Street, named for the territory's first surveyor, was the centerpiece of Clark's Las Vegas townsite. At its end stood the grand new railroad station, backed by 63 acres of prime real estate owned by the railroad. In addition to metal and welding shops for train repairs, the property even included a roundhouse, a circular workshop with a giant turntable used for fixing locomotives.

In May 1905, regular train service to the Clark Townsite ushered in a new era.

Las Vegas was born on May 15, 1905 at an auction around a platform erected under Mrs. Stewart's giant mesquite tree. Buyers who didn't camp out on her old ranch in advance arrived by rail on auction day, with the train fare deducted from the purchase of a Las Vegas lot. Entrepreneurs, railroad speculators, investors and merchants — nearly 3,000 people in all — gathered to hear railroad representative C.O. Whittemore explain the developments planned for the area.

The Stewart ranch had been measured and carved into 40 blocks that were subdivided into 1,200 parcels and cleared of brush and mesquite trees. There would be a plumbing system that would pressurize the water on every lot, plus graded streets and enough businesses and shops to support a community employing several hundred men.

The auction went on for two days under full sun, in 110-degree heat. By the end of May 16, the land that cost Senator Clark $55,000 was sold at auction for a total price of $265,000.

Early investor Ed Von Tobel later recalled the 1905 auction in a newspaper story commemorating the city's 50th anniversary: He came away with two small $100 lots. The total down payment was $50, but the railroad credited him with $22, the price of his train ticket to Las Vegas. (A $22 train ticket in 1905 would cost about $550 today.)

Not everyone was thrilled. J.T. McWilliams, who had reserved some of his 80 acres nearby for commerce, tried to attract businesses away from the Clark Townsite, but competition was futile. The train completely bypassed the McWilliams Townsite, and the natural topography, with a steep dip and a curve, made it just about impossible for pedestrians to

Hotel Las Vegas, circa 1905

reach the other side of the tracks. On Clark's side, with the train station
and Fremont Street, businesses profited not just from train travelers on
rest stops, but from an entire town of railroad workers with money to
spend. Sadly, the McWilliams Townsite remained a Ragtown.

The promises made by Clark's company were honored; construction
in Las Vegas began immediately. On the morning of May 17, tents,
lumber and other building materials were hauled enthusiastically to
sites throughout the new town. The tents housed a post office, saloons,
gambling houses, a bank and a hotel. By nightfall, buildings stood in
various stages of completion. By mid-June, roofs went onto stores and
houses. The Las Vegas Land and Water Company, a subsidiary of the
railroad, graded and oiled 10 miles of city streets, built concrete or
wooden curbs throughout the town and brought water to every lot.

Water also flowed to the railroad station for steam engines and train car maintenance. Work began on a residential plumbing system, a collection of redwood pipes bound with wire and then tarred together, in September. A celebration arose when water pipes began serving Miller's Hotel on the southeast corner of Fremont and Main streets, across from the train station.

The Armour & Company ice plant and icehouse that served the railroad, the town and even outlying mining areas, set up shop in a building painted bright yellow. Everyone in town knew where to find it.

Electricity arrived in 1906, and in 1907 the electric company began providing telephone service too. Electricity was only available at night, and the phone only worked in the daytime, before 8 p.m.

From day one, prostitution was legal in Las Vegas, with its own designated district just one block from the train station. Blocks 16 and 17 (today's First through Third street, between Stewart and Ogden avenues) were zoned for saloons and brothels, frequently the site of fistfights, shootings and drunken brawls. Gambling was legal too, until Nevada enforced an anti-gambling law in October 1910. The railroad paid its employees through direct deposits at local banks just to make sure that wages weren't squandered at a gaming table on payday.

As the train prospered, so did the town, but the trainmen were also responsible when things went wrong. At the train station, there was filtered, softened water, since impurities like sand could damage the steam engines. Residents in the outlying town faced tougher prospects. A clogged wooden pipe could shut down the water to a whole block for days. When it was flowing, residents complained of dead flies and other bugs in the water.

As author Florence Lee Jones reported in *Water, A History of Las Vegas*, one company spokesman stepped forward to admit that little fish might occasionally make it through the water system's filters, "but even this cannot in any way injure the water or make it filthy."

With its rugged terrain and unyielding climate, Nevada remained one of the least-developed states in the nation. However, in 1909, Nevada redistricted its territories to include a new county with a rapidly expanding population. Las Vegas became the seat for the newly organized Clark County, named for the Montana senator who built the railroad that employed that expanding population.

The town of Las Vegas officially incorporated in 1911. Ten years later, Harriman's company, the Union Pacific, absorbed the San Pedro-Los Angeles and Salt Lake Railroad. The town was stable, but it wasn't immune to economic tides, since everyone's fortunes depended upon one railroad.

The railroad put the town on the map—and kept it there.

1. Rail Station: Main Street at Fremont
2. McWilliams Townsite
3. Clark Townsite
4. Miller's Hotel: Southeast corner of Fremont and Main streets
5. Block 16: First through Second streets, from Stewart to Ogden avenues
6. Block 17: Second through Third streets, from Stewart to Ogden avenues
7. Hotel Las Vegas: Stewart Avenue at Main Street

■ Existing Building
■ Building No Longer Exists

CHAPTER 4.

RAGTIME VEGAS

William A. Clark and his railroad advisors instantly acquired hundreds of partners with a stake in Las Vegas's future when they auctioned the first properties in 1905. No one could predict who the winning bidders would be, what skills they might bring, and what demands. Now, an entire urban infrastructure was needed. Schools, fire department, medicine and commerce—the new citizens had to invent it all.

Meanwhile, ragtime was the innovative new music gaining popularity across the nation in the first years of the 20th century. Las Vegas residents were singing new tunes too, for everything, starting with their very presence, was new. Together, they faced a bold new challenge: learn how to harmonize as a community. Fast.

Because of the extreme climate, the fire department was a primary concern. At first, almost the entire population lived in canvas tents that were illuminated by kerosene lamps and heated by stoves fueled with gasoline. When the desert winds raged, a tent could go up in flames within seconds if the canvas touched a stove or a lamp. Then, the flames swept rapidly to neighboring tents if the wind was strong.

← (top) Las Vegas and the Union Pacific Railroad depot, circa 1909
(bottom) Fremont Street, circa 1920

Las Vegas, 1910

Las Vegas residents assembled an all-volunteer fire department. Its equipment consisted of an old ranch wagon and a hose fitted with a clay pipe that served as a makeshift nozzle; firemen didn't even have a bell or a siren. Instead, when a fire broke out, everybody grabbed their guns, ran out into the street and fired into the air to sound the alarm.

With few trees and no tall buildings to obscure the view, the volunteer fire crew didn't need to report to a firehouse. When they heard the shots, they scanned the horizon and headed directly to the source of the smoke.

However, the firemen quickly discovered that the wooden pipes installed by the railroad to deliver water to residents couldn't provide the kind of water pressure required to put out a fire, and fire hydrants were scarce. Instead, the blacksmith made large metal hooks that were attached to the ends of some redwood poles. When a fire broke out, firemen used the long-armed hook to snag a corner of the burning tent, then pulled it away from the others. Firefighters saved the other tents by pulling the flaming canvas into the road where it could be extinguished.

Eventually, a six-foot-tall metal triangle was installed on Fremont Street (where Binion's Gaming Hall and Hotel stands today), with a giant bolt attached by a string. When a fire broke out, the sound of that bolt pounding on the giant triangle served as the fire alarm that sent

volunteers running. In 1912, the fire department finally got its first specialized hose cart and a 500-foot hose.

There were perks for volunteer firefighters in early Las Vegas. After a fire, every bar in town offered free booze to any man wearing a fireman's coat.

With no city government in place when Las Vegas was settled in 1905, there was no mechanism to levy taxes to fund a school. The first public school in Las Vegas was built with private funds, as parents pooled their resources to educate their children. And there was no time to lose. Just weeks after the auction in May, residents chose a school board and put them to work. For $700, townspeople bought the four-room Salt Lake Hotel and renovated it. The first school year started on October 2, 1905, with two teachers and nearly 60 students. Two weeks later, enrollment had grown to 81. Teachers taught all subjects to six grade levels, dividing the time to roughly 15 minutes per class per subject. All students heard the lessons being taught to the other grades.

Finally, in 1910, the railroad's Las Vegas Land and Water Company donated an entire city block (from Fourth Street to Fifth Street, between

Clark and Bridger avenues) on which a two-story school with 14 classrooms would be built. With much pomp, the cornerstone was laid for the new school during the railroad's Fourth of July celebration that year. They even buried a small time capsule with the names of all the students. Weeks later, disaster struck. Before the new building was completed, the existing schoolrooms burned down! For the following year, the children went to school in the Methodist church and part of a nearby rooming house.

Then, the newly constructed school stood vacant for months while the contractor argued with the school board's inspector. The new school would be the first building in Las Vegas to have indoor staircases. But, in a town with a justifiable fear of fire, those staircases were made of wood. Classrooms on the second floor were death traps. The school session didn't begin in 1911 until after the contractors completed concrete steps outside the building that reached the second story.

That outdoor staircase came in handy, frequently serving as the stage for special events. Most school and civic programs took place on the schoolhouse steps.

In the days before refrigeration, residents shopped for groceries almost daily, but the sun (and the dust, and the flies) made that a challenge. Instead, vendors traveled from house to house. The Las Vegas butcher traveled from door to door every morning taking orders, then returned in the afternoon to deliver pork chops, steaks and hamburger meat as ordered. Peddlers sold most goods to women, from eggs and milk to pots and pans, door to door, while most men labored at their jobs on the railroad.

The iceman was the most popular vendor with children. He knew who had an icebox, and the shape of the ice block it required. Long before the invention of the Popsicle, children sucked on the shards of ice that fell from the iceman's wagon as it rattled through the unpaved streets.

By 1910, Las Vegas had a population of 945, but no sewage system. Surprisingly, it was Sewer Bonds that motivated the citizens of Las Vegas to incorporate as a city, for only a formalized local government could sell bonds to finance its construction. On March 16, 1911, Las Vegas was incorporated, in part, to end the makeshift cesspools.

In that first election, the men of Las Vegas elected Peter Buol, a former railroad cook, to be the first Mayor, along with four City Commissioners. (Women didn't win the right to vote in Nevada elections until 1914.) With basic services and a government in place, Las Vegas came of age in the ragtime era. Its residents proved that they could harmonize in the desert.

1 First Fire Alarm: 128 Fremont St.
2 First Schoolhouse: Southwest corner of Second Street and Lewis Avenue
3 First Permanent School Building: block from Fourth Street to Fifth Street, between Clark and Bridger avenues

■ Existing Building
▨ Building No Longer Exists

CHAPTER 5.

LEGAL TENDER

In the 1920s, the going rate for a girl on Block 16 was $3.

There was foreplay first, of course: a girl in a bar would dance with a customer for one dollar. Then he'd buy her a drink for 50 cents. He drank the hard stuff, she drank tea or water; then they'd adjourn to a room upstairs and complete the transaction.

Prostitution was legal, matter-of-fact and public in Las Vegas, in its own authorized zone downtown. Before auctioning the residential lots, the railroad bosses designated Blocks 16 and 17 for establishments that sold liquor. (It's today's First through Third streets, from Stewart to Ogden avenues.) Both blocks were lined with saloons, but Block 16 was taller: it had second-story hotel rooms where travelers slept and working girls plied their trade.

In 1905, the clever railroad bosses inserted a temperance clause in the deeds for all the real estate they sold in Las Vegas, prohibiting liquor in any place but Blocks 16 and 17. It guaranteed a vibrant and boisterous business district, conveniently located near the train station.

← The bar from the infamous Arizona Club

The Red Rooseter Nightclub, Bock 16, 1940s

Many of the local prostitutes were independent contractors, without pimps. Each working girl negotiated the price of a room for the day (perhaps for a cut of earnings), and took her place on the saloon's front porch, wearing something scanty (Western-style shirts were always popular). As part of the deal with the saloon-owner, deals were never finalized until the gentleman spent some money at the bar. Plus, she kept the dollar from that dance, and got back 25 cents from the price of that drink the gentleman bought. Best of all, the work was steady.

Air conditioning wouldn't arrive for 40 years in Las Vegas, and in the daytime desert heat, its streets looked uninhabited. But at night, Block 16 was packed. Riots, shoot-outs and fistfights erupted regularly.

The only women permitted inside the saloons and gambling clubs that lined Block 16 were prostitutes. Those who preferred the protection of a madam worked in bordellos in exchange for a cut of the night's profits. They received weekly medical examinations, and not just for venereal diseases. Tuberculosis was a common affliction among miners in Nevada. Their mouth-to-mouth contact with prostitutes could spread the bacteria rapidly.

The classiest place on Block 16 was the Arizona Club—once located at 219 North First Street, but now long gone—with a bar and wainscoting of carved red mahogany, and a beveled glass front door. Constructed with remarkable speed, it opened on March 31, 1906, less than a year after the railroad auctions. Illuminated by gaslight, the club offered roulette, blackjack tables, nickel slot machines and a sloe gin fizz for 15 cents. In 1912, when the new owner built the second story, he added a bordello upstairs. The Arizona Club became known as the Queen of Block 16, the most popular bar-casino-brothel in Las Vegas.

Black men were permitted to conjugate only with black hookers, but the same wasn't true for white men. More than one bordello employed black girls for a white-only clientele.

PROSTITUTION GETS PUSHED OUT

Eventually, the streetwalkers and bordellos were deemed too raw for the wives and girlfriends who accompanied their men on gambling vacations. The sex trade was becoming a nuisance. In 1941, when the U.S. Army planned to open Nellis Air Force Base just 15 miles from downtown, military brass informed city officials that Las Vegas would be off limits to military personnel if prostitution remained.

Smelling money from a new direction, the City Commissioners admitted that Las Vegas could no longer afford to defend the brothels. In a very public show of force on December 2, 1941, 16 officers, including the police chief and the police commissioner, arrested 22 women on prostitution charges. On January 6, 1942, the City Commissioners voted to rescind the liquor licenses and slot-machine licenses for all the saloons on Blocks 16 and 17. Without those reliable sources of income, the saloons and brothels soon closed.

During World War II, the worn-out buildings became cheap rooming houses. Finally, in January 1946, the city declared the old structures to be hazardous. Blocks 16 and 17 were razed, erasing every trace of the bawdy businesses that once thrived there. Parking structures were erected on the site of Blocks 16 and 17 where they remain to this day, behind Binion's Hotel and Gambling Hall.

Today, prostitution is against the law in Las Vegas, though it remains legal in other parts of the state.

Monday was banking day for working girls. After a profitable weekend, dressmakers were kept busy too. One old-timer described the madams and their brothels as "decorous. They operated as they knew they must. Their word was good; their credit was good. Other than the association of prostitution and sin, I would say they were excellent members of the community."

From the actions of this very first generation of landowners, Las Vegas was memorable for its vices. As early as 1906, Las Vegas was known as Sin City. Yet what some might judge to be sinful, the citizens of Las Vegas respected as legitimate businesses. It's the model that's kept Las Vegas afloat ever since.

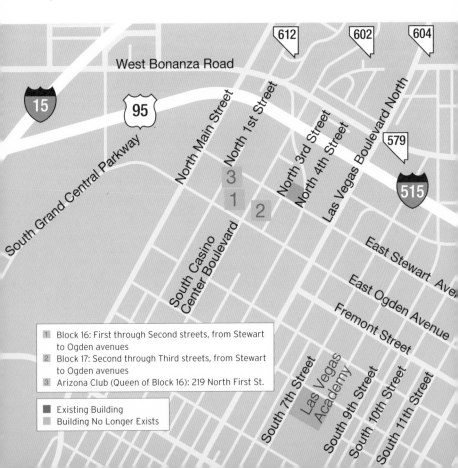

1 Block 16: First through Second streets, from Stewart to Ogden avenues
2 Block 17: Second through Third streets, from Stewart to Ogden avenues
3 Arizona Club (Queen of Block 16): 219 North First St.

■ Existing Building
■ Building No Longer Exists

CHAPTER 6.

HOOVER DAM

For its first 70 years, Nevada had the lowest population in the United States, for it lacked the natural resources to develop like other states.

The fortunes of early Las Vegas were tied to the railroad, its sole industry. To encourage more commerce, local commissioners permitted frontier town vices to lure more people to Nevada. Quickie weddings and fast divorces, alcohol and prostitution—services that were shunned in priggish America were sources of income for desert towns.

Economic salvation came in December 1928, when President Calvin Coolidge signed the bill authorizing the construction of a massive dam on the Colorado River. The shocked citizens of Nevada erupted in jubilation. School closed early. Adults and children joined together in an impromptu parade down Fremont Street. Barely 30 miles from downtown Las Vegas, the new Boulder Dam was a game-changer.

Since 1910, dam projects had been under consideration along the Colorado River. Promising studies of the Black Canyon and Boulder

Canyon increased the project's potential and scope: the roaring river could generate power to the vast expanse of Nevada, Arizona and California, with Lake Mead serving as a gigantic reservoir. Water would finally come to the desert communities in torrential volume. Authorizing the dam was the final flourish to the Coolidge presidency; 10 months later, with Herbert Hoover as president, America's economy collapsed in the Great Depression. It was President Hoover, in July 1930, who signed the appropriations bill that put Americans to work building the nation's infrastructure.

These were the Prohibition years, when liquor was against the law in America. Though transactions became shadier and the moonshine was possibly lethal, Las Vegas saloons survived, and so did the sex trade. Hungry for a new form of legitimate business, Las Vegas commissioners temporarily closed some of the seedier establishments, hoping to present a respectable community when Secretary of the Interior Ray Wilbur dropped in to inspect the dam site.

Commissioners promoted the city as being ideally situated for Boulder Dam's administration and employee housing. But Wilbur saw through the plan when a federal employee among his entourage returned to the train smelling of liquor, regaling all with his adventure at the Arizona Club. Wilbur denounced the vices of Las Vegas. The Department of the Interior would support the construction of a federally controlled town adjacent to the worksite.

And controlled it was. Twenty miles away, Las Vegas's new neighbor was Boulder City, a fenced-in community with a guard at the gate, created as part of the Boulder Canyon Project Federal Reservation. It was a 144-square-mile enclave that included the dam site, the future reservoir and spacious stretches of territory around the town. The rules were strict: Whites only, no gambling, no prostitution and absolutely no liquor.

← Workers put a coat of paint on the Hoover Dam, circa 1946

The first grocery store in the new Boulder City settlement, 1931

Fifty-two miles of railroad track were installed between Las Vegas and the dam site to haul construction materials. At first, Boulder City was just a collection of bunkhouses attached to the canyon wall, built by the company to house 480 single men until the accommodations were constructed. Then came eight large dormitories made of plasterboard. Sixteen hundred workmen soon called it home, thankful for a job and a roof at a time when many Americans were starving.

Work began in March 1931 when the construction contract was awarded to Six Companies, Inc., a consortium of firms hired by the U.S. Bureau of Reclamation to build the dam. Secretary Wilbur called the project Hoover Dam, in honor of the sitting president. At nearly $49 million it was the largest labor contract ever issued by the U.S. government.

An estimated 42,000 unemployed men from across the country descended on southern Nevada, desperate to land one of the 5,000 jobs building the Hoover Dam. They arrived in railroad boxcars and jalopies, on horseback, and even on foot. The population of Las Vegas suddenly swelled from 5,000 to 25,000 residents. The contract forbade "Mongolian" (Chinese) labor on the project, and it would be almost two years before the first 10 black men were hired, at 50 cents an hour. Like the other black workers, they had to commute 30 miles in each direction from the Westside of Las Vegas.

African-Americans were crammed along the dusty paths of the Westside. Squatters filled shantytowns in the territory that would later become North Las Vegas. The influx brought prosperity to the local economy, but it came at a huge cost to the local government, which strained to accommodate the sanitation, utilities, health, housing and education needs of the surging population.

Then, state legislators ratcheted up the excitement. On Monday, March 17, 1931, within days of work commencing on the Hoover Dam, Nevada reaffirmed its reputation as the nation's

HOOVER VS. BOULDER

In September 1930, Secretary of the Interior Ray Wilbur named the Hoover Dam, following the tradition of naming dams after presidents. Herbert Hoover had been in office for only 18 months, and the economy was in ruins. Was Wilbur paying back his Republican crony?

Although some of the dam's construction transpired while Hoover was in office, he hadn't been involved in its planning or in its eventual delivery. Hoover was an unpopular, one-term Republican president, perceived to be out of touch with the workingman during the Depression. Shantytowns called "Hoovervilles" popped up in many parts of the country, sad clusters of homeless Americans seeking shelter.

Defending his choice, Wilbur described Hoover as "the great engineer whose vision and persistence . . . has done so much to make [the dam] possible.."

Partisan critics scoffed that "the 'great engineer' had quickly drained and ditched and dammed the country."

Since Congress hadn't ratified the Hoover Dam moniker, when Democrat Franklin D. Roosevelt was elected in 1932, his administration attempted to quell the controversy. In 1935, in the ceremony marking the dam's completion, FDR praised the magnificent engineering feat of the Boulder Dam.

The public wasn't so sure. The names were used interchangeably and no one seemed to mind. Finally, in 1947, President Harry S. Truman (another Democrat) signed a bill that passed both houses of Congress by a unanimous vote: if the dam must be named for a president, then the name of the dam must be: Hoover.

rogue state. Since games of chance were illegal everywhere in the country, Nevada's lawmakers chose to make a lucrative leap: in the depths of the Depression, they legalizing casino-style gambling. Within months, Fremont Street was lined wall-to-wall with gambling joints. Penny slot machines showed up in almost every gas station and grocery store across the state. Large-scale gambling took root in Las Vegas. Gaming redefined the city, making it a destination, not just a train stop. The city would now grow at an exponential rate. With a wink to its Boulder City neighbors, Las Vegas billed itself as the "Best Town By A Dam Site."

Miners were some of the first men to be hired, for they were already braced for the dirty, dangerous, backbreaking work ahead. The men were rowdy and profane, but also relentless workers. With three shifts in daily rotation, a non-stop rivalry developed between crews working in different tunnels and among the three shifts to see who could drill the fastest, fire the most blasts, and advance the farthest in an eight-hour period. It's no surprise that the workmen were equally competitive when it came to carousing in the streets of Las Vegas.

These men lived for payday. With money in their pockets, they raced out of Boulder City, heading directly to that two-block stretch of Fremont Street and Block 16, where they encountered one of the most spectacular concentrations of wide-open vice to be found anywhere in Prohibition America. Las Vegas was a party: a bawdy, brightly lit assemblage of gambling dens, bordellos and saloon after saloon, even during Prohibition.

Meanwhile, powerful Democratic senators channeled some New Deal funds into Las Vegas: Fremont Street became the town's first paved road. Funding also expanded Las Vegas's sewer system, installed its first traffic light and built a park, golf course, convention center and a public school. Today that school is a national landmark.

As Depression-era Americans yearned for good news, the Hoover Dam delivered. In newsreels and speeches, the federal government touted the Hoover Dam as the Eighth Wonder of the World. It became a magnet for tourists, attracting over 100,000 people during its construction phase. (Visitors spiked to 300,000 in 1935, the year the dam opened.) Most of those visitors, of course, stopped in Las Vegas to witness and partake of its unique attractions. Welcoming the tourist trade, Las Vegas now billed itself as "The Gateway to the Boulder Dam," as the project was then called.

In 1935, President Franklin D. Roosevelt presided over the ceremony that marked the completion of the dam. For four and a half years, laborers had spent their days drilling into the walls of hard, stubborn rock or pouring tons of concrete. In summers, the heat averaged above 110 degrees each day; sometimes the stone was literally too hot to be touched. One hundred men per day might collapse from heat exhaustion, but they were promptly replaced from among the thousands waiting for a chance

VISIT THE HOOVER DAM

By 1939, the Hoover Dam was putting out the equivalent of 1,835,000 horsepower; about 64 percent went to California, with the remainder split between Arizona and Nevada utility companies. To this day, the dam remains an important source for water and energy for the Southwest.

Nearly 1 million visitors tour the Hoover Dam each year, and millions more drive across it. The Bureau of Reclamation has conducted tours through the Hoover Dam and power plant since 1937. It is open to visitors every day of the year except on Thanksgiving and Christmas Day.

Location:
The dam is located 30 miles southeast of Las Vegas on US Highway 93 at the Nevada-Arizona border.

For tour information visit usbr.gov/lc/hooverdam

See the Hoover Dam from the river with rafting trips through the Black Canyon on the Colorado River. For information visit blackcanyonadventures.com.

To learn more about Boulder City, visit the Boulder City Museum, bcmha.org.

to work while squatting in Las Vegas. By the time construction was finished, 112 workers had died. The Six Companies delivered its project to the United States two years and two months ahead of schedule.

Within months, thousands of dam workers were gone. Fremont Street was suddenly empty. But Las Vegas didn't revert to being just a railroad stop again. Thanks to the construction of the dam, locals had tasted the potential for profit in America's forbidden desires. Now, they'd just need to lure people to the desert.

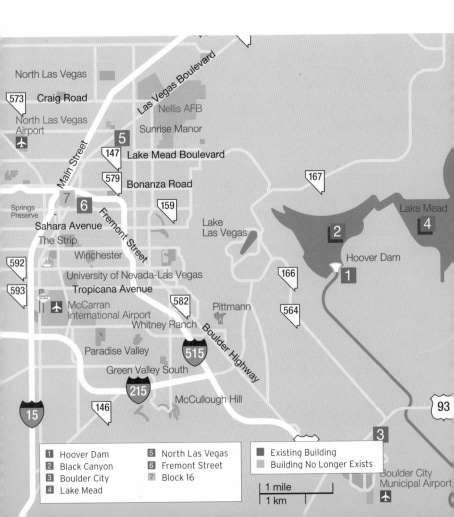

CHAPTER 7.

THE ORIGINAL WISE GUY

Tony Cornero arrived in Las Vegas directly from prison.

At age 25, while living in San Francisco, the Italian immigrant became a millionaire by using his "shrimping business" as a cover for the much more profitable enterprises of smuggling Canadian whisky to ports along the California coast. Things went so well that he expanded his fleet and began importing rum from Mexico. But that's where he got caught. In 1926, federal agents found more than 1,000 cases of rum from Mexico on Cornero's shrimping vessel. At his sentencing, Cornero, the original wise guy, told reporters he'd only purchased the illegal cargo "to keep 120 million people from being poisoned to death."

Out of jail in 1931, he joined his brothers Frank and Louis in Las Vegas. Just six weeks after gambling was legalized in Nevada, Louis Cornero secured one of Las Vegas's first gaming licenses. The brothers agreed that former felon Tony would run their club in Las Vegas, though his name could not appear on the club's license.

Tony Cornero (second from left) and others gambling aboard the ship *Lux* off coast of California, 1946

The Corneros invested $31,000 to build the Meadows, one of the earliest hotel-casinos on Fremont Street. Located far from the brothels on Block 16, the Meadows aimed to attract a classier crowd. It had 30 hotel rooms with running water, plus a nightclub with its own house band. Most importantly, the Meadows was one of the first casinos to be built for legalized gambling. The county granted it a license for two craps tables, two roulette wheels, two blackjack tables, two poker tables, one hazard table, one faro table and five slot machines.

The Meadows was immediately hailed as one of the most attractive establishments in town, a departure from the saloons along Fremont Street. However, the star attraction at the Meadows was reputed to be its liquor; Tony Cornero imported real Canadian whisky while his competitors served up gin made in Las Vegas bathtubs.

He hired squeaky-clean acts to perform in the nightclub as a cover for the club's illegal liquor sales. One of the first shows presented at the Meadows: the Gumm Sisters, three singing girls, direct from their Hollywood debut in a series of one-reel movie shorts. The youngest, a 9-year-old billed as "Baby Gumm," would soon gain fame in the movies, under a new name: Judy Garland.

There was plenty of gambling in Las Vegas in the decades before Nevada made it legal. The Race Wire, a telegraph service that delivered horse racing results to bettors across the nation, was a big moneymaker for New York crime boss Meyer Lansky. To oversee the Race Wire in the west, he deployed his boyhood pals Bugsy Siegel to Los Angeles and Moe Sedway to Las Vegas.

These Race Wire proprietors resented the intrusion of Cornero's conspicuous casino. They knew that legalized gambling was a game-changer; it lured their customer base in new directions. Lansky's Syndicate tried to muscle in, demanding a percentage of Cornero's gaming profits. When Cornero refused to comply, the Meadows was burned to the ground in September 1931, allegedly torched by New York mobsters.

Cornero sold his Las Vegas interests after the disaster in the desert, and returned to business on the sea. Rechristening himself "Admiral" Tony Cornero, he purchased two large ships that he converted into luxurious floating casinos. He anchored his gambling ship the *S.S. Rex* just three miles offshore from Santa Monica, and the *S.S. Tango* offshore at Long Beach, California. Floating in international waters, Cornero could run a casino without interference from U.S. authorities. The *S.S. Rex* carried a crew of 350, including waiters and waitresses, gourmet chefs, a full orchestra and a squad of gunmen. Its casino could accommodate over

2,000 gamblers. From the Santa Monica Pier, wealthy patrons from Los Angeles and Beverly Hills hopped into water taxis for a 10-minute trip to the ships. Once again, Cornero was reaping cash.

It outraged California Attorney General Earl Warren. He ordered a series of raids on the ships, with comical results. When law enforcement attempted to board his vessels, Cornero fended them off with fire hoses. One standoff lasted for nine days before Cornero finally gave himself up. As he surrendered, the wise guy quipped: "I have to get a haircut, and the only thing I don't have aboard this boat is a barber."

Warren was not amused. When the Coast Guard seized the *S.S. Rex* in 1939, the "Admiral" was long gone. Cornero had moved the party back to Las Vegas, where he leased the entire ground floor of the Apache Hotel and Casino on Fremont Street and opened a new club, christened the S.S. Rex.

1. The Meadows: Fremont Street and Boulder Highway
2. Block 16: First through Second streets, from Stewart to Ogden avenues
3. Apache Hotel and Casino / S.S. Rex Club: 128 Fremont St.
4. Stardust: 3000 Las Vegas Blvd. South
5. Desert Inn: 3145 Las Vegas Blvd. South

■	Existing Building
■	Building No Longer Exists

CORNERO'S LAST ACT: THE STARDUST

Tony Cornero continued to dream big, but a plan to invest in Baja California, Mexico, went horribly awry. One night, two Mexican men came to Cornero's Beverly Hills home and shot him four times in the stomach. He underwent surgery and survived.

His brush with death did not diminish his zeal for business. Soon after his recovery in 1954, Cornero went to work on a new Las Vegas resort. He paid $650,000 for 32 acres on the Strip and sold shares, intent on building the largest and plushest hotel in the world. He named it: the Stardust.

By now, Cornero had begun to believe his own hype, imagining that his past was forgotten or forgiven by authorities. Shortly after construction began, Cornero's bootlegging conviction caught up with him: the Nevada Gaming Commission denied his application for a license. Cornero owned a half-built casino that he was not allowed to operate.

Offering the half-built Stardust hotel as collateral, he secured loans from Moe Dalitz, who had bailed out Wilbur Clark's Desert Inn, and from Meyer Lansky in New York, the same mobster who allegedly torched the Meadows two decades earlier. Despite the cash infusion, Cornero ran out of money again.

On July 31, 1955, he asked his investors for $800,000 more, to stock the casino with cash. Hours later, while playing craps at the Desert Inn, Cornero dropped to the floor and died.

Was Cornero's drink poisoned? His body was removed from the casino floor before the coroner or the Sheriff's Department was contacted. His cocktail glass was washed before the sheriff's deputies could examine it. No autopsy was performed; a coroner's jury in Los Angeles, 300 miles away, determined that Cornero died of a heart attack.

Cornero was buried at Inglewood Cemetery in Los Angeles, a short distance from the pier where water taxis once raced to the *S.S. Rex*. He was 55 years old.

Dalitz immediately took charge of the resort. At the opening on July 2, 1958, the Stardust was celebrated as the largest hotel in the world, with the most luxurious casino on the Las Vegas Strip, just like Cornero dreamed it would be. Governors and senators, local officials and Hollywood celebrities attended the opening day festivities at 3000 Las Vegas Boulevard South.

When it opened, the Stardust was the largest hotel in the world, with 1,065 guest rooms. It featured the largest casino in Las Vegas, the largest lobby and the largest swimming pool. It even had a drive-in movie theater in back. For 10 years, the showroom at the Stardust hosted one of the most successful performers in Las Vegas history: singer Wayne Newton.

Cornero, the hotel's founder, is credited with the lucrative concept of placing slot machines in the hotel lobby, now a mainstay at many gambling establishments.

In the end, the Stardust couldn't compete with the mega-resorts springing up everywhere on the Strip, with thousands more rooms to accommodate the large groups that attend conventions. Newer hotels assumed the titles as largest and plushest.

On Tuesday, March 13, 2007, the Stardust resort was imploded. It was a grand ceremony that included fireworks.

CHAPTER 8.

MARILYN PLAYS VEGAS

Norma Jeane Baker was born in Los Angeles and became Marilyn Monroe in Hollywood. But she never would have gotten there without a stop in Las Vegas that allowed her to follow her dreams.

Norma Jeane Baker was 16 when she married a Merchant Marine named Jim Dougherty in 1942. The newlyweds were separated for months at a time as Jim's career took him to distant places during World War II. He left teenage Norma Jeane alone in their Hollywood home, so she got a job in a Los Angeles munitions factory.

A photographer on assignment asked her to pose for *Yank*, a military magazine. Weeks later, 18-year-old Baker's photos reached the Blue Book Agency, the top modeling agency in Hollywood. Blue Book got her pinup photos into more magazines. Suddenly Norma Jeane was a model.

When Jim Dougherty returned, he was furious. "It's your career or me" he's reported to have said. Baker's modeling appointments irritated him,

← Norma Jeane Baker, the future film star Marilyn Monroe, sand skiing on a dune, circa 1942

and he just couldn't rationalize the costs of a model's hair care, wardrobe and makeup. When Dougherty departed on the next long excursion with the Merchant Marines, Baker knew what she had to do. She packed her bags and headed to Las Vegas.

Back in 1931, Nevada relaxed the divorce laws. According to the new law, anyone who resided in Nevada for six weeks could seek a divorce in a Nevada courtroom. On May 14, 1945, Baker arrived at the home of Minnie Willett, the aunt of her foster mother, at 604 ½ South Third Street, for the sole purpose of establishing residency. The next step in her career would be to divorce Jim Dougherty.

On June 1, she marked her 20th birthday in Las Vegas. Six weeks later, on July 5, *Norma Jeane Dougherty v. James Edward Dougherty* was filed in Clark County court. Baker completed her six-week residency, with Aunt Minnie as her witness, then returned to Hollywood.

On July 16, Baker performed a screen test at the offices of Twentieth Century Fox. Studio chief Darryl Zanuck was so dazzled by her sex appeal on celluloid that he offered her a contract for $75 a week. On August 26, she signed the deal. She met with Ben Lyon, the casting agent at Fox, and together they devised her new name: Marilyn Monroe.

On September 13, 1946, Baker was back in Las Vegas, this time at the courthouse. She took the witness stand and swore under oath that she had lived on Third Street from May 14 to July 5, and that she always intended to make it her "permanent place of residence."

It was perjury. She had no intention of making a home in Nevada. With a job waiting at a Hollywood movie studio, lying under oath was just another Las Vegas gamble to the newly minted Monroe. The judge let it ride. Her crime was no more egregious than what thousands of other divorcées were doing in Nevada, swearing allegiance and then skipping town. The judge granted a decree of divorce.

Today, Marilyn Monroe is revered in Las Vegas, where impersonators, shop windows and even Madam Tussaud's Wax Museum pay tribute to her memory.

Her stay was very brief, but it was the first step on her road to stardom. Besides the courthouse, Marilyn Monroe never performed in Las Vegas.

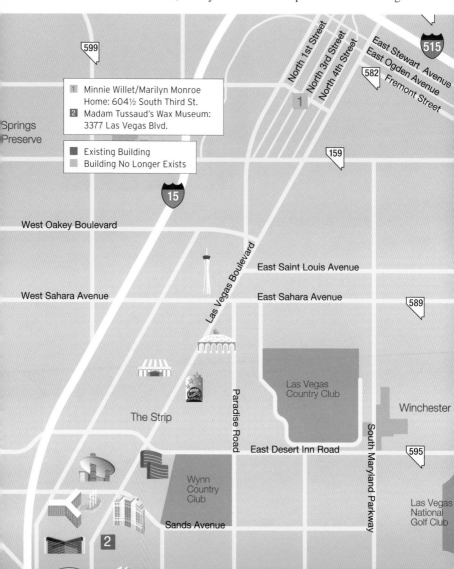

1 Minnie Willet/Marilyn Monroe Home: 604½ South Third St.
2 Madam Tussaud's Wax Museum: 3377 Las Vegas Blvd.

■ Existing Building
■ Building No Longer Exists

MARRIAGE, LAS VEGAS STYLE

Marilyn Monroe isn't the only person who has taken advantage of Nevada's loose laws regarding marriage and divorce.

In Las Vegas, marriage is like craps: a roll of the dice available 24 hours a day, seven days a week.

Why is the city such a popular site for weddings?

Nevada was one of the first states not to require a blood test or a waiting period prior to that walk down the aisle. While most states today have abandoned the blood tests (once a common requirement to determine if potential parents might pass on a disease), many states demand a waiting period of one to five days between the issuance of the marriage license and the actual ceremony.

Not in Las Vegas, where compulsion rules. In the city with no clocks, there's never a reason to wait. With about 120,000 ceremonies performed annually, the wedding industry is a huge and competitive business, from grand-scale productions at the costliest resorts to drive-thru windows where commitments roll out fast.

Prices range from as little as $55 (for a no-frills, non-religious "desk wedding" performed at the Office of Civil Marriages, just a block and a half from the Marriage License Bureau) to elaborate fantasy events.

Want to be wed on a 16th century British "throne" or get dressed like Tarzan and Jane? You can do them both at the Chapel of Love on the Las Vegas Strip. Need to get married by "Elvis Presley"? There's the Graceland Wedding Chapel on Las Vegas Boulevard or the Elvis Chapel on South 9th Street.

Forgot your ring, veil, tux, witness, photographer or limo? That and plenty more can be provided by every chapel...for a price.

WHO SAYS "I DO" IN LAS VEGAS?

Frank Sinatra and Mia Farrow
50-year-old Frank married 21-year-old Mia in a private ceremony at the Sands on July 19, 1966. Two years later, Sinatra had divorce papers served to Mia while she was on the set of *Rosemary's Baby*.

The Seven Brides of Mickey Rooney
Starting in 1944, actor Mickey Rooney exchanged nuptial vows eight times, with seven of those events occurring in Las Vegas. The shortest stint lasted 100 days. His longest marriage is with his current wife Jan Chamberlin, whom he wed in 1978.

Axl Rose and Erin Everly
At 4 a.m., the Guns N' Roses star reportedly proposed to Ms. Everly (daughter of famed singer Don Everly) by saying, "Marry me or I'll kill myself." They were promptly wed on April 28, 1990 at Cupid's Wedding Chapel on Las Vegas Boulevard. Three weeks later, Rose filed for divorce, then reconciled, then had the marriage annulled one year later.

Dennis Rodman and Carmen Electra
The 37-year-old basketball star wed the *Baywatch* beauty at the Little Chapel of the Flowers on November 15, 1998. When they sobered up, they ended their marriage nine days later.

Angelina Jolie and Billy Bob Thornton
With "Billy Bob" tattooed on her arm, Angelina marched down the aisle for the second time (it was the fifth marriage for Billy Bob). The couple wore blue jeans in their ceremony at the national landmark Little Church of the West on Las Vegas Boulevard on May 5, 2000. They were divorced in 2003.

Britney Spears and Jason Allen Alexander
The two 22-year-olds were married spontaneously at the Little White Wedding Chapel at about 5 a.m. on January 3, 2004. The bride, wearing jeans and a baseball cap, was walked down the aisle by a hotel bellman. The couple signed annulment papers just 55 hours later.

Nicky Hilton and Todd Andrew Meister
With her sister Paris as a witness, socialite Nicky married money manager Todd at the Vegas Wedding Chapel while in town for a celebrity poker tournament. Paris's dog Tinkerbell wore a tiara to the event at 2:30 a.m. on August 15, 2004. The couple was granted an annulment eight weeks later.

Paul Newman and Joanne Woodward
Not every celebrity wedding ends in annulment. One week after divorcing his first wife, 33-year-old Newman married 27-year-old Woodward at the El Rancho on January 29, 1958. Their loving union lasted 50 years, until Newman's death in 2008.

CHAPTER 9.

FIRST HIGH ROLLER

W.R. "Billy" Wilkerson thrived on risk; he never went anywhere without a pair of dice in his pocket. He took the high-stakes route to satisfy his compulsive gambling; along the way, he invented modern Las Vegas.

The son of a professional gambler, Wilkerson fell in love with risk while in medical school. When he won a large bet on the 1916 World Series, he acquired half-ownership in a Nickelodeon in Fort Lee, New Jersey. That fateful bet ended his medical training, immersing Wilkerson in the burgeoning movie industry. When Hollywood invented talking pictures in 1927, Wilkerson saw an opportunity: the market for a publication devoted solely to moviemaking.

Wilkerson took another big gamble. He packed his wife and his mother in a flivver and drove across America to seek a new career in Hollywood. On September 3, 1930, the first issue of *The Hollywood Reporter* published by W.R. Wilkerson, Jr., arrived on newsstands. It eventually became known as "the Industry Bible," required reading for everyone employed in the film industry.

Billy Wilkerson's partners Gus Greenbaum and Moe Sedway of El Cortez, with an unknown friend

With the *Reporter's* profits growing, Wilkerson gambled obsessively. He'd rent private planes bound for Reno, or find his way to the "gambling shacks" on Fremont Street in Las Vegas. He gambled every day, planning his business meetings around daily treks to the local racetrack at Hollywood Park or to gaming ships moored beyond the three-mile limit. Over the years, his compulsion alienated wives in five failed marriages. Wilkerson was hooked; gambling delivered an adrenaline rush that rivaled any other conquest.

Wilkerson developed his sophisticated taste on trips to Europe during Prohibition. He rolled the dice in Monte Carlo and dined at Parisian supper clubs. Surveying Hollywood in 1934, he noted the absence of sophisticated nightspots. Glamorous movie stars, famous producers and directors all earned plenty of money, yet there was limited elegance in Hollywood. With the end of Prohibition, Wilkerson expanded his business into a string of glittering nightclubs: the Vendome, Café Trocadero, LaRue and, most notably, Ciro's, which became the best places for celebrities to be seen. Of course, columnists from *The Hollywood Reporter* supped at Ciro's too, ready to scoop every new story.

In 1944, Billy Wilkerson, the impeccably dressed power player from Hollywood, obsessive gambler and owner of every elegant club on the Sunset Strip, figured it out: The winning gambler is on the other side of the table. Wilkerson reversed his role as a gambler. He'd wager the money he would otherwise spend on his gambling habit to build a club of his own in Las Vegas.

Sizing up the competition, Wilkerson decided that those "shacks" were the problem. The country-Western ruggedness, with sawdust on the floor, was too downscale. To lure high rollers out of their Beverly Hills mansions, he'd need to provide something fantastic, more than just another casino. He'd create a *resort*, a self-contained oasis in the desert, combining all the elements he loved best: the crisp efficiency of a hotel on the French Riviera, an elegant restaurant like his glittering Hollywood nightspots, a show room, a pool with cabanas and best of all, a casino with the black-tie sophistication he'd found at the tables in Monte Carlo. Wilkerson would mix European refinement with Hollywood glamour in the desert. His resort in Las Vegas would be a destination for every star in Hollywood; they'd want to read about themselves in *The Hollywood Reporter*.

In 1945, Wilkerson paid $84,000 for a 33-acre corner lot that he spotted on the way to the Las Vegas airport. It was miles away from the commercial district around Fremont Street, which would distinguish his venture from the cowboy casinos. With the design team from Ciro's,

Wilkerson planned a massive complex: 250 hotel rooms, more than the two largest downtown hotels combined, plus restaurants, a theater, a pool, gym, spa and a nine-hole golf course. Waiters in black-tie. Racy showgirls that rivaled the Folies Bergère. No clocks and no windows, because daylight breaks a gambler's concentration, something Wilkerson knew first-hand. And an irresistible amenity found no place else: air-conditioning, guaranteed to keep gamblers at the tables and drinkers at the bars. Wilkerson created the model for all the Strip hotels that followed. This was the birth of modern Las Vegas.

One of Wilkerson's favorite New York City hangouts was the Stork Club. It inspired him to name the Las Vegas enterprise after another long-legged bird: the Flamingo. He even envisioned live flamingoes roaming the lawn at the completed resort. Budgeted at $1.2 million, Wilkerson raised half the funds for the Flamingo from Bank of America. Then he convinced Howard Hughes, whose movie studio advertised heavily in *The Hollywood Reporter*, to pay $200,000 in advance for advertising. That money went into the construction capital fund too.

Since he'd never run a casino before, Wilkerson recruited two silent partners: Gus Greenbaum and Moe Sedway, who ran the very successful El Cortez casino on Fremont Street. They agreed to secure all the necessary gaming permits and oversee the daily operations of the casino for a percentage of the gambling profits. It seemed practical to hire "the boys," as Wilkerson called the two young hucksters who were 25 years his junior, yet knew more about the Nevada Gaming Commission than he did. It was a decision Wilkerson would regret. At the time, though, it sounded great: the boys knew how to run a Nevada casino, and Wilkerson knew how to open a stylish club with a celebrity clientele. How could it miss?

Construction started in November 1945 but shut down in January 1946 because Wilkerson, the high roller, was still short by $400,000. He had gambled the construction capital and lost it all.

The building's foundation and one-third of its framework baked in the desert sun for a month as he toyed with the idea of scaling down the project or dumping it altogether. Then the boys placed the phone call that changed Las Vegas.

The Syndicate, Meyer Lansky's organized crime partnership with the Genovese crime family, owned the El Cortez, and Greenbaum and Sedway worked for him. Lansky was already profiting from the El Cortez and he saw the new casino's potential for wealth. The boys brought him the deal: $1 million would complete the Flamingo's construction. Lansky could bail out Wilkerson by becoming his partner.

This time, Lansky figured it out. With that elegant Hollywood publisher as their front, the whole sprawling enterprise was legit. With little exposure, he could control the biggest casino at the classiest joint in Las Vegas. If Wilkerson provided the class, Lansky would provide the capital.

Days later, while Wilkerson toured the half-baked project with his builder, a very gracious attorney unexpectedly arrived at the site.

He was G. Harry Rothberg, a former bootlegger from Chicago. On Lansky's behalf, counselor Rothberg offered Wilkerson the best possible option: For the money needed to finish construction, Lansky's Syndicate would own two-thirds of the Flamingo. Wilkerson would own all the land and retain one-third ownership if he agreed to manage the Flamingo.

The investors wished to remain silent partners; Wilkerson would continue to make all creative decisions, and Lansky would pay all the bills. On February 26, 1946, Rothberg and Wilkerson signed a contract conveying 66 percent of the Flamingo to Lansky and his syndicate of investors. One week later, a check for $1 million arrived at the offices of W.R. Wilkerson Enterprises. The deal was on.

Construction resumed within days. Wilkerson was elated, and saw himself again as the proud innovator of the new Las Vegas, talking up the project among his Hollywood cronies and publishing stories about it in *The Hollywood Reporter*.

One month later, the boys arrived at the site with a loudly dressed young man, a face that Wilkerson knew too well from his nightclubs and gossip columns. He was Benjamin "Bugsy" Siegel, now retained by the Syndicate as Lansky's representative. Despite his notorious crime record, Siegel was Wilkerson's new partner.

Now comes the card shark's nightmare: trapped in a game of his own creation from which he cannot escape. To Billy Wilkerson, the compulsive gambler, the table just got very cold.

1 The Flamingo
3555 Las Vegas Blvd. S.
2 El Cortez
600 E. Fremont St.

Existing Building
Building No Longer Exists

CHAPTER 10.

BUGSY

In 1920s parlance, acting crazy meant going "bugs." Teenage punks on New York streets knew that gang member Benjamin Siegel was downright bugsy: they'd often seen his psychotic temper flare. To the underworld, that could also be an asset. But that hot temper would lead to his undoing in Las Vegas.

At age 15 in 1923, Brooklyn-born Benny Siegel dropped out of eighth grade so that he and his friend Moe Sedway could run a protection racket. New York's pushcart merchants had to pay these little bandits a dollar a day, or their merchandise would be incinerated overnight.

Benny and Moe soon joined 19-year-old Meyer Lansky in guarding the trucks that transported bootleg liquor. They worked for Arnold Rothstein, the renowned mobster who had recently been tried for bribing the Chicago White Sox in the 1919 World Series. While protecting Rothstein's booze in 1924, 16-year-old Siegel killed an attempted hijacker, establishing his reputation as a hot-tempered gunman and intimidator. Benny was bugsy all right, though no one dared say it to his face.

← Bugsy Siegel, 1940

Rothstein diversified into illegal horse-race gambling, controlling the Racing Wire, a service that relayed horserace and prizefight results and sporting events scores to off-track bookies across the country.

When Rothstein was shot and killed in 1928, the business was redistributed. Lansky inherited the Racing Wire, which he expanded into new cities. When Nevada became the first state in America to actually legalize the Racing Wire, Lansky sent Sedway to oversee operations in Las Vegas. In 1935, 29-year-old Bugsy left his wife and kids in Brooklyn to manage the illegal Racing Wire in Los Angeles. It was estimated to generate a half-million dollars a day.

Living out a fantasy as a Hollywood hotshot, Siegel soon rubbed elbows with studio heads, movie stars and entrepreneur Billy Wilkerson. Siegel became a regular at Ciro's, Wilkerson's celebrated nightclub on the Sunset Strip. His photo appeared in *The Hollywood Reporter* as he escorted starlets like Ava Gardner, Betty Grable, Lana Turner and aspiring actress Virginia Hill. Siegel even fantasized about an acting career, paying for headshots and a screen test, but no Hollywood decision-maker took the brutish Siegel seriously as an actor.

Siegel and Sedway both told their boss Lansky that there was money to be made in Las Vegas. It was still basically a one-horse town, little more than a train depot with some low-rent gambling saloons. But the potential was huge: liquor was legal again, and two new Defense installations had just been built on the outskirts of town, bringing hundreds of men and their paychecks to the Fremont Street saloons. With the country at war, thousands of anxious couples were crossing the Nevada borders to be wed in a state that didn't require blood test results like everyplace else. Newlyweds needed a place to stay. Plus, Las Vegas was already renowned for its quickie divorces. Siegel predicted that Fremont Street would soon be packed beyond capacity. Now was the time to invest in Las Vegas.

Back in New York, Lansky had become friends with Charles "Lucky" Luciano, soon to become head of the Genovese crime family. Their alliance, known as the "Syndicate," merged New York's Jewish mafia with one of the infamous "Five Families" of Italian-American gangsters. Their handshake agreement gave birth to a cooperative venture for investments.

Over the next few years, with Lansky's guidance, Siegel tested the Las Vegas market with $3 million from the Syndicate, earned from narcotics trafficking and other illegal actions. He invested the Syndicate's money in gambling halls on Fremont Street and bought the profitable, four-year-old El Cortez outright in 1945. The official owner was a front man, but the investors were the biggest bosses in organized crime.

It was easy to understand the Mob's interest in casinos: it's a cash business. In a casino's hard count room, a gangster could simply stride in with a bag or a box, skim cash profits off the top, then walk out the door. As long as the money kept pouring in, the counters looked the other way. When the opportunity arose to invest in the Flamingo hotel and casino, the New York gangsters could practically smell the cash.

Situated in the barren desert, the Flamingo was beyond Las Vegas city limits in the unincorporated town of Paradise, Nevada. That made it beyond the reach of the city's Slot Tax too. (In fact, the famed "Las Vegas Strip" actually lies completely outside of the Las Vegas city limits, in Paradise and the neighboring town of Winchester)

Already partially constructed, the Flamingo was a full-fledged resort on a scale that dwarfed the other casinos, with a swimming pool, a parking lot for L.A. commuters and, of course, the biggest, swankiest casino in town, ripe for the Syndicate's skim. Lansky stayed out of town, but at Siegel's urging, the Syndicate assumed two-thirds control of the Flamingo on February 26, 1946.

Bugsy Siegel couldn't completely forsake his Hollywood lifestyle, but to oversee the completion of the Flamingo, he moved into the Last Frontier hotel in Las Vegas. In a breathtaking turn of events, Benjamin Siegel, a wise guy from the underworld, would now be a partner of the man whose Hollywood success story he admired most: Billy Wilkerson.

CHAPTER 11.

THE FLAMINGO

Even on paper, the Flamingo looked like a game-changer. The bold venture could turn dusty old Las Vegas into a glamorous destination, but conflicts between the partners overseeing its construction were apparent from the outset.

The Flamingo was stamped with Billy Wilkerson's imprint. When its construction was completed, the publisher of *The Hollywood Reporter* had access to the A-list Hollywood celebrities that would fill the place. Meanwhile, Bugsy Siegel's wise guys were looking to skim money from the casino's nightly haul. While Wilkerson envisioned a Las Vegas version of his star-studded Ciro's nightclub, Siegel planned secret passageways that led to a waiting getaway car.

Wilkerson introduced Siegel to his team of professionals: architects, builders and designers who patiently educated the gangster on how to construct the resort. But this new persona was not an easy fit. Siegel soon grew jealous of Wilkerson's talent and vision. He became a cocky know-it-all, making decisions without Wilkerson's authorization, informing work crews that Wilkerson put him in charge, then ordering changes that

The interior of the Flamingo

conflicted with the drawn plans. It was soon apparent to all that Siegel had no idea what he was doing.

To keep the peace, Wilkerson suggested that they divide the responsibilities in half: Siegel would oversee the hotel construction, and Wilkerson would take care of the rest. Within a month, Siegel had spent all the money allocated for the entire hotel, and now demanded money from Wilkerson's budget too. When Wilkerson refused to comply and advised him to stick to the plans, Siegel went over his head, back to his boss Meyer Lansky in New York.

It was May 1946. Wilkerson hoped that Lansky's Syndicate would see the cost overruns and replace Siegel with someone rational, who understood the scope of the project. Instead, Siegel announced to the Syndicate that the original agreement was flawed. It needed to be altered to give him complete control of the Flamingo. Amazingly, Lansky complied; the Syndicate turned over the entire Las Vegas venture to an eighth-grade dropout, the novice Bugsy Siegel. Wilkerson, who still owned the land, was reduced to the role of shareholder; his creative involvement ended abruptly.

A new player entered the story, silently. When FBI Director J. Edgar Hoover learned that Siegel had gained control of the Flamingo, he instructed FBI agents to tap Siegel's phones and bug his suite at the Last Frontier. Over the next year alone, the FBI would amass a 2,400-page file on the actions of Mr. Benjamin Siegel.

At the construction site, Siegel was manic, demanding high-end materials when America was still emerging from wartime shortages. He insisted on the most expensive marble imported from Italy. He didn't like Wilkerson's windowless casino; he demanded the demolition of a concrete wall to be replaced by a picture window facing the pool. Costs soared. By October 1946, with the project nowhere near completion, the Syndicate had invested over $4 million.

Siegel installed his girlfriend Virginia Hill, a former actress, as the Flamingo's interior decorator. She was clueless. He'd leave her in charge for days at a time as he searched for new investors, and then he'd return to review her decisions and undo them. When Hill installed costly new drapes in the main lounge, even inexperienced Siegel could see that they were highly flammable. The drapes were sent back to Los Angeles to be chemically treated for fireproofing. They were a pair, Bugsy and Virginia, building, demolishing and then rebuilding every element within Wilkerson's design.

The Syndicate was sinking millions into a grandiose and unproven scheme, helmed by a guy that everyone knew was bugsy. The investors began to exert pressure: they wanted to be paid. Without informing the Syndicate, Siegel sold non-existent stock to new investors, then used

The Flamingo at night

their cash to continue construction. He doubled the workforce, hoping to cut his construction time in half, but all it did was increase his labor costs. The Syndicate demanded a balance sheet, but Siegel couldn't deliver it without revealing he had oversold the shares.

When Hill took not one, but two, ill-timed vacations to Europe, the Syndicate lost its remaining shred of faith in Siegel. How could the project once budgeted at $1.2 million cost this much money? They suspected that Siegel and his girlfriend were skimming construction funds, making deposits in a Swiss bank account, preparing for a getaway.

Amid the noise and anger, Wilkerson remained the project's largest shareholder. As the value of the enterprise increased with each new cash injection, the value of Wilkerson's shares increased too. That's when Siegel announced it was time to convene a meeting of all shareholders.

With a representative for Nevada's Lieutenant Governor Clifford A. Jones acting as his attorney, Siegel delivered the news to Wilkerson and his attorney Greg Bautzer: "I've sold 150 percent of this deal, but there's only 100 percent, so everybody's gonna have to cut, including Billy."

The furious exchange that followed was ended by Wilkerson's attorney, who informed everyone present that he was filing an affidavit with attorneys general in California and Nevada and the FBI, disclosing Siegel's remarks about selling fraudulent stock. Wilkerson would make no cuts to his legal share of the enterprise. Then Bautzer chided Siegel's attorney: "If Mr. Siegel and his associates are wise, they better make sure that Mr. Wilkerson doesn't accidentally fall down a flight of stairs. They'd better make sure he doesn't sprain his ankle walking off a curb, because that affidavit is going to be in the hands of those men. So they'd better be goddamned sure Mr. Wilkerson enjoys a very long and happy life."

The FBI was listening. When J. Edgar Hoover leaked a few facts about the Flamingo to Walter Winchell, the hugely popular gossip columnist and radio announcer, listeners across the nation heard: "According to the FBI, a prominent West Coast racketeer is endeavoring to muscle a prominent West Coast publisher out of his interest in a West Coast hotel."

The Syndicate investors, accustomed to deals made out of the spotlight, witnessed wildcat Bugsy Siegel attracting far too much attention, threatening the loss of the Flamingo's gaming and liquor licenses. Now the whole nation knew that the FBI was watching. It was time for investors to exert more pressure.

Wilkerson, now in fear for his life, sailed to Paris, where he checked into the prestigious Hotel George V under a pseudonym to keep his whereabouts hidden. He entrusted *The Hollywood Reporter* and his clubs on the Sunset Strip to his attorney, editors and managers, who maintained the businesses in his absence. Wilkerson submitted his daily editorial to *The Hollywood Reporter* by telex or by dictating it over the phone to uphold the illusion that he was still at his desk in Hollywood.

From Wilkerson's earliest plans, the Flamingo's opening date had always been set for March 1, 1947. To start repaying the Syndicate, Siegel decided to open early. He picked December 26, 1946, a desperate move by a desperate man. Although the hotel was incomplete, he hoped the casino's income over New Year's Eve might generate enough capital to appease the investors.

That didn't happen. Opening night was a fiasco. The weather was so severe that air traffic was grounded. Howard Hughes provided two chartered planes to transport the Hollywood crowd to Las Vegas, but they never got off the tarmac.

Instead of Hollywood celebrities, the place was packed with curiosity-seekers, and a curiosity is exactly what they got. Wilkerson had recruited the staff from his clubs on the Sunset Strip and planned a black-tie gala for opening night, but Siegel omitted that little detail from the invitations. Now, as the local cowboys piled in, they were startled to see starchy croupiers in white ties and tails. Patrons accustomed to chatty waitresses in local restaurants were put off by the formal service from waiters in tuxedos. Perhaps the biggest affront to the locals: Instead of a familiar cowboy welcoming them at the front door, the gentlemen of Nevada were instructed to remove their hats while they were indoors.

Jimmy Durante, Xavier Cugat and Rose Marie were the headliners in the show room; they were major stars in 1946 who filled the place for the first two nights. By the third night of their two-week engagement, there were only nine or 10 people in the dining room. With no hotel rooms available, gamblers cashed in their winnings and went to the casinos where their hotel rooms awaited. At the end of the first week, Siegel tallied up the casino's balance sheet in horror: it was $275,000 in the red.

He closed the Flamingo, vowing not to re-open until all construction was complete.

The Flamingo reopened on March 1, 1947, the originally scheduled date. Similar to a Miami Beach hotel, the entire expanse had wall-to-wall carpeting—no sawdust here—plus stylish, modern furniture, dramatic lighting and air-conditioning. Gone were the stuffy white ties on the dealers and waiters. High rollers from Hollywood and Beverly Hills arrived in increasing numbers. By May, the Flamingo was finally making a profit, but the Syndicate members, who had waited impatiently for this day to come, began to assemble a list of Siegel's infractions. At $6 million, the Flamingo was the most expensive hotel ever constructed.

Still hiding in Paris when the Flamingo opened, Wilkerson was scared straight of his compulsive gambling. He lost control of the most monumental deal of his gambling life; now it was time to fold. Wilkerson returned to the United States, then on March 19, 1947, he executed a document that released his ownership in the Flamingo. At age 57, the compulsive gambler figured things out anew: the only way to win is not to play the game.

Wilkerson gave up gambling for the rest of his life.

On June 20, 1947, while Virginia Hill was on another excursion to Europe, Siegel stayed at her rented house in Beverly Hills. As he read the *Los Angeles Times* near the undraped front window, a gunman hiding behind a rose bush in the front yard fired nine shots through the window. The marksman hit Siegel twice in the heart and twice in the head. The impact was so great that it blew his left eye out of its socket. Benjamin Siegel, the gangster from New York, died in Beverly Hills at age 41.

The funeral was held on June 22. Despite the many people Siegel knew in California and Nevada, only five attended the ceremony. Today, his remains lie in a crypt at the Hollywood Forever Cemetery in Los

The slain body of Bugsy Siegel on a sofa in his Beverly Hills home, 1947

Angeles. On New York's Lower East Side, his family of orthodox Jews had his name engraved on a memorial plaque at the Bialystoker Synagogue. In 1993, when the final wall of the original Flamingo was demolished, a plaque was erected in Bugsy's memory in the garden of the renovated resort. Since then, guests and staff have reported sightings of a ghostly presence nearby, as well as in the hotel's wedding chapel and Presidential Suite.

Years after the murder, the FBI determined that Lucky Luciano placed the hit on Siegel. Following the disastrous opening in December, the Syndicate investors were furious about their losses at the Flamingo but knew they couldn't kill Siegel until after construction was complete.

Twenty minutes after Siegel was shot to death in Beverly Hills, "the boys," Moe Sedway and Gus Greenbaum, announced to the staff at the Flamingo: "We're taking over here." A chapter ended.

Over the next seven years, Greenbaum turned the Flamingo into an enormously profitable enterprise for the Syndicate. The responsibility also fell to the boys to produce a detailed accounting. The mess they uncovered came as no surprise: Crooked contractors and unpaid builders had swindled Siegel, who was too disorganized to notice. To pay them, Siegel oversold the project by nearly 400 percent.

The Flamingo's historic significance surpasses all the bad blood that went into its construction. The Strip now had its foundation. Wilkerson proved that an upscale casino could flourish in the desert; resorts based on his model would make Las Vegas an international destination.

But more hoodlums had to arrive first.

The Strip

Winchester

Springs Preserve

Las Vegas Country Club

Wynn Country Club

Winchester Community Center

Las Vegas National Golf Club

University of Nevada-Las Vegas

McCarran International Airport

Jaycee Park

Hadland Park

Natu Park

Paradise Park

West Bonanza Road
West Jackson Street
East Bonanza Road
West Bonneville Avenue
West Charleston Boulevard
East Charleston Boulevard
West Oakey Boulevard
East Saint Louis Avenue
West Sahara Avenue
East Sahara Avenue
East Desert Inn Road
Sands Avenue
East Flamingo Road
East Harmon Avenue
East Tropicana Avenue

North Main Street
North 1st Street
North 3rd Street
North 4th Street
Las Vegas Boulevard
Paradise Road
South Maryland Parkway
Spencer Street
East Stewart Avenue
East Ogden Avenue
Fremont Street
South Arville Street
South Valley View Boulevard

95
15
515
159
3
579
582
589
595
592
593

1 mile
1 km

1	The Flamingo:	3555 Las Vegas Blvd. S.
2	Last Frontier:	3120 Las Vegas Blvd. S.
3	El Cortez:	600 E. Fremont St.

Existing Building
Building No Longer Exists

CHAPTER 12.

ESTES KEFAUVER

There was a presidential election coming in 1952, and Senator Estes Kefauver had high aspirations. Prior to launching his campaign, he seized the national spotlight by leading the Senate's first investigation into organized crime. His committee focused in on Las Vegas gangsters.

Senator Kefauver recognized that the new experiment called television was here to stay. Not only would the Kefauver Committee interrogate gangsters, they would interrogate them on live television. *The Senate Special Committee to Investigate Crime in Interstate Commerce* was television's first reality show.

Throughout his political career, Kefauver, a Democrat from Chattanooga, Tennessee, supported regulations that kept any entity from gaining too much power. Favoring the little guy, he had introduced legislation that made the prosecution of big corporations easier. After 10 years of pushing his anti-monopoly bills in the House, Kefauver was elected to the U.S.Senate in 1948, where his star continued to ascend. In 1950, *Time* magazine labeled him "one of the Senate's most valuable ten," and "a most effective symbol of the South's new progressivism."

Such praise motivated Kefauver to greater conquests. With an eye on the White House in the upcoming election, the Kefauver Committee would hold hearings in 14 cities, including Las Vegas.

By 1952, there were about five million televisions in American homes, entertaining and informing 20 million Americans daily. Even though television broadcasts occurred for just part of the day, the medium's potential was apparent to everyone. No postwar home was complete without one. Now, Kefauver's organized crime investigations would make television history, as the first time regularly scheduled programs were pre-empted to televise live news events.

To those with televisions, the investigation had great weight simply because there were so few choices among channels. For many viewers, it was the first time they had heard that crime might be organized nationwide. As Kefauver declared in a newsreel: "Organized crime operates on a syndicated basis across state lines in the United States that is a much bigger, more sinister, and larger operation than we had ever suspected." Despite the primitive production values of Kefauver's broadcasts, the senator's hype kept viewers watching. Who wouldn't want to see the "sinister" element taken down by a United States senator on live TV?

At first, the spotlight worked. Throughout the summer and early fall of 1951, the publicity generated by Kefauver and his national broadcasts shuttered illegal gambling dens and similar enterprises across the country. Their wary operators waited to see what might come next. New York crime boss Frank Costello covered his face, infamously refusing to be seen on television. Former New York Mayor William O'Dwyer, then serving as the U.S. Ambassador to Mexico, saw his career go to ruin when the Kefauver Committee summoned him back to New York. His association with organized crime figures hounded him for the rest of his life.

← Virginia Hill, girlfriend of Bugsy Siegel, testifies before Estes
Kefauver's special committee on organized crime in 1951

Kefauver showboated through it all, delighted that television was making him a household name. During the hearings in 1951, he even appeared as a celebrity guest in the first season of the quiz show *What's My Line?* Kefauver's prospects for the White House were improving with each successive TV appearance.

But Kefauver's high-flying plans came to a crash in Las Vegas, where local laws proved to be the Committee's undoing. While Kefauver had anticipated revelations from witnesses in this notorious city, hours of testimony produced no hard evidence. In fact, the Committee uncovered no wrongdoing whatsoever. Casinos in Las Vegas were legal, gaming was a recognized industry and casino operators had the full sanction of the state. End of story. To many, Kefauver suddenly appeared to be a buffoon…on live, national television.

Kefauver's fumble in Las Vegas was a clarion call to every criminal who had just been squeezed out of business in another city. Come to Las Vegas, where your sordid past might actually be an asset. As one wise guy cracked: "I love that man Kefauver. When he drove me out of an illegal operation in Florida and into a legalized operation in Nevada, he made me a respectable, law-abiding citizen. And a millionaire."

Kefauver's Committee heard testimony from over 600 witnesses nationally, but gained little traction. Many of the witnesses were high-profile crime bosses, but Kefauver caught not one of them. The organized crime hearings became a transitional point in Kefauver's career: the invincible politician proved to be fallible after all. His Senate colleagues realized that taking down organized crime would require a more serious effort, perhaps from someone with inside knowledge.

Nonetheless, the groundwork had been laid. As expected, Kefauver declared his candidacy in the 1952 election, but failed to win the Democratic nomination. Four years later, he campaigned again and wound up as the vice-presidential running mate of Democratic nominee

Adlai Stevenson. They ran against incumbent President Dwight D. Eisenhower and lost by a large margin.

Kefauver, a heavy drinker and smoker throughout his life, suffered a heart attack on the floor of the Senate in 1963. He died two days later at the age of 60.

CHAPTER 13.

ATOMIC LAS VEGAS

Bikini Island is nowhere near Las Vegas, but for a brief time in the 20th century, the two locations shared an explosive history.

Scientists knew little about nuclear fallout when the first atomic bombs were dropped over Hiroshima and Nagasaki. After the war, President Harry Truman created the Atomic Energy Commission to study nuclear energy. A test site was established on the remote Bikini Atoll, a group of 23 islands in the western Pacific Ocean, part of the Marshall Islands, a U.S. Trust Territory after World War II.

Pat McCarran, Nevada's longtime senator (from 1932 to 1954), was incensed. Why was the U.S. spending money to blow up the Bikinis when they could be employing Americans at home?

To bring jobs to the desert, Senator Pat McCarran lobbied President Truman and the Atomic Energy Commission. He and Governor Charles Russell pointed to the vast, arid wasteland in Nevada and encouraged its use for nuclear testing.

← Operation Hardtack, De Baca Test, Nevada Test Site, October 1958

The "MET" (Military Effects Test) shot, Operation Teapot, conducted at the Nevada Test Site, April 15, 1955

They got their wish. The Nevada Proving Grounds was inaugurated on January 11, 1951, an area 150 square miles larger than the entire state of Rhode Island. Nuclear testing on North American soil began on January 27, 1951, when the Commission tested a one-kiloton bomb code-named "Abel."

The nuclear flash in Nevada could be seen from as far away as San Francisco. The *Las Vegas Review-Journal* reported the sighting of a mushroom cloud about 65 miles northwest of Las Vegas. The U.S. government actually thought they could keep it a secret. When the *Review-Journal* published the news of a second sighting, FBI investigators arrived at the editor's office, suspecting that someone had leaked security secrets from inside.

No one had, of course. With the arrival of nuclear tests nearby, Las Vegas had one more reason to crow. Any town can shoot off a few fireworks, but here in Las Vegas? We've got the atomic bomb!

The Chamber of Commerce began to publish the schedule for nuclear experiments, and the whole town went a little crazy. Las Vegas, the city that once billed itself as the Gateway to the Boulder Dam, now branded itself The Atomic City.

Guests could plan their visits to coincide with scheduled detonations. Clark County changed its official seal to the image of a mushroom cloud. The Sands Hotel staged beauty pageants to select "Miss Atomic Bomb," the Flamingo's beauty parlor offered an Atomic Hairdo and every bartender in town learned how to mix an Atomic Cocktail.

> **ATOMIC COCKTAIL**
>
> Ingredients
> 1 ½ ounces vodka
> 1 ½ ounces brandy
> 1 teaspoon sherry
> 1 ½ ounces Brut champagne
>
> Instructions
> Stir the vodka, brandy and sherry with cracked ice, then strain into a chilled cocktail glass.
>
> Add 1 ½ to 2 ounces cold champagne.

Senator McCarran was continually grateful for the federal funds that were pumped into Nevada as a result of the Proving Ground. In 1952, Governor Russell gushed: "It's exciting to think that the sub-marginal land…is furthering science and helping national defense. We had written off that terrain as wasteland, and today it's blooming with atoms."

Businesses continued to boom. Hotel restaurants in Las Vegas started selling Atomic Lunchboxes to guests who wanted to drive closer to the reservation for a picnic and a better view. The new Atomic View Hotel even promised views of the bomb's mushroom cloud from its swimming pool.

While the detonations were frivolous fun for Las Vegas, what the Atomic Energy Commission was learning with each new blast was important,

AFTER THE ATOM BOMB

In 1979, the *New England Journal of Medicine* first reported significant numbers of leukemia deaths of children in the counties of nearby Utah that were exposed to high fallout between 1959 and 1967.

In 1982, a lawsuit was brought by nearly 1,200 people who accused the government of negligence at the Proving Grounds, causing leukemia and other cancers. In 1984, a federal judge ruled that the government was negligent, exposing thousands of people downwind from the Test Site to radioactive fallout. The Centers for Disease Control estimated that 11,000 people died from diseases directly related to nuclear test fallout.

In 1997, the Radiation Exposure Compensation Act permitted people living downwind of the Nevada Test Site who suffered from cancer or other serious illnesses to receive compensation of $50,000 each. By January 2006, over 10,500 American claims had been approved, totaling over $525 million in compensation.

"Sober" is rarely used to describe Las Vegas. However, with the tragedies in downwind Utah as perpetual reminders, Las Vegans knew they had dodged a deadly bullet.

but horrific. Entire "doom towns" were built on the reservation: roads paved, houses furnished, refrigerators stocked; a town populated by mannequins.

Then a bomb would flash. Next, scientists observed how far the mannequins shattered, or which building materials fared best.

In another test, 111 pigs were attired in uniform fabrics with seams, zippers and drawstrings to determine the best field jackets for the U.S. Army; 72 animals died on impact.

In Operation "Buster," the government sent 5,000 troops on a training mission, pursuing a hypothetical army after detonating a nuclear device. The troops charged through the radioactive fallout in the hours immediately after its detonation.

In May 1953, an aboveground nuclear blast code-named "Harry" spread radioactive fallout across the continent. It destroyed film being manufactured at the Kodak laboratories in faraway Rochester, New York.

The Atomic Energy Commission expanded its research, continuing to test in the Marshall Islands. Bikini remained ground zero for at least 20 more aboveground tests through 1958.

Meanwhile, hundreds of protests occurred in Nevada. Many activists labeled themselves "downwinders," because the winds placed their homes, schools and businesses in the path of the nuclear fallout. They fought against the secrecy at the Proving Ground, where anybody could learn the schedule but nobody heard about the risks to the populations nearby. Supporters of the tests called themselves "Cold Warriors," believing like Senator McCarran that they were helping to fight off a nuclear threat from the Soviet Union.

President John F. Kennedy, the only president ever to visit the test site, terminated the testing, with the first in a series of nuclear test ban treaties signed by a succession of presidents. On July 17, 1962, "Little Feller" was the last aboveground test in Nevada. In all, 100 nuclear tests were conducted aboveground; testing continued underground for decades to follow, expanding the nuclear workforce to some 12,000 people during the 1970s, the program's busiest years.

Renamed the Nevada Test Site, underground experimentation bloomed further during President Ronald Reagan's Star Wars initiative, but by then nobody in Las Vegas saw much reason to celebrate, as the dangers of radioactive fallout became common knowledge. The last test in Nevada took place on September 23, 1992.

In 1994, U.S. President Bill Clinton and Russian President Boris Yeltsin met in Moscow and issued a joint statement: "For the first time since the earliest days of the Nuclear Age, the two countries will no longer operate nuclear forces, day-to-day, in a manner that presumes they are enemies."

Two years later, leaders from 71 nations at the United Nations General Assembly and signed the Comprehensive Nuclear-Test-Ban Treaty, an

THE ATOMIC MUSEUM

The Atomic Testing Museum, displays the whole atomic past from the earliest Nevada tests through the present. Exhibitions revisit the giddy era of "Atomic Las Vegas" and its dark lingering cloud.

The Atomic Testing Museum
755 East Flamingo Rd.
Las Vegas, NV 89119
Museum Store: 702-794-5150
www.atomictestingmuseum.org

The Atomic Testing Museum is open to the public seven days a week:
• Mon-Sat 10 a.m. - 5 p.m.
• Sunday noon - 5 p.m.

Last Ticket Sold at 4 p.m.

Closed Thanksgiving, Christmas Day and New Year's Day.

agreement to ban nuclear explosions worldwide in all environments. By 2011, 153 countries had ratified the treaty, though it has yet to enter into force.

After 1,021 official tests in Nevada, Las Vegas gave up the Atomic City moniker, and the mushroom cloud came off the Clark County seal.

Most telling: it's hard to find a bartender who can still mix an Atomic Cocktail.

1 Nevada Test Site
2 Area 51
3 The Sands: 3355 Las Vegas Blvd. S.
4 The Flamingo: 3555 Las Vegas Blvd. S.
5 Atomic Testing Museum: 755 E. Flamingo Rd.

■ Existing Building
■ Building No Longer Exists

CHAPTER 14.

THE OTHER SIDE OF THE TRACKS

The Westside was barely a mile from Fremont Street, but it was a distant world. Known as a dirt-poor shantytown for decades, it evolved into Las Vegas's thriving African-American community in the 1940s and '50s. Today it's known as Uptown, the Historic Westside.

When J.T. McWilliams bought an 80-acre parcel of land from the U.S. government in 1904 (today it's Bonanza Road to Washington Avenue, from D Street through H Street), he thought he'd get rich by selling it off as individual lots near the railroad that would soon be built across the property. But the train bypassed the McWilliams Townsite, stopping at the intersection of today's Fremont and Main streets, where the new train station was the focal point of downtown Las Vegas.

Businesses on the eastern side of the tracks prospered in the new town. On the other side of the tracks, hope faded fast. The unpaved terrain was too rough to move building supplies, so the new owners constructed makeshift housing with canvas and cardboard. The Westside became known as "Ragtown," a pejorative name shared by several shantytowns throughout the area.

A game of craps at the El Morocco Club on the Westside of Las Vegas, the final night before the casino's closing, 1954

By the 1930s, the construction of Hoover Dam attracted many more laborers to the area, including African-Americans seeking work. But Jim Crow laws were observed across Nevada; Las Vegas was a segregated city. When African-Americans arrived seeking work on the railroad, they were immediately directed to the Westside, giving birth to a sad American idiom. In Las Vegas, black people could only reside "on the other side of the tracks."

As the black population swelled, the rules seemed to constrict. "No Coloreds Allowed" became the policy at every hotel and casino in Las Vegas; blacks could only enter as laborers. Many worked in the mines

An undated photograph of patrons at a Westside casino

outside of Las Vegas, or as railroad hands and porters on the expanding railroad. Regardless of where they worked, almost all people of color returned to the same Westside shantytown each night.

It was nearly impossible for African-Americans to own a home in the early 20th century. Banks and mortgage companies would not lend money to blacks for housing or businesses, especially not in an undesirable location like the dirt-poor Westside. A few daring souls ventured east of the tracks; they purchased properties at the railroad auction in Las Vegas, where they opened businesses that catered to a black clientele. Jake Ensley founded the Oklahoma Café; Mammy Pinston opened the Plantation Kitchen that was famous for its Southern fried chicken. Ensley opened a second restaurant across the street from the bordellos on Block 16. Uncle Jake's Barbeque became a favorite hangout, where men could feast on barbecued ribs outside while ogling the hookers who strolled through the business district.

When Hoover Dam was completed in 1936, unemployment soared. Some African-Americans were fortunate to be employed by local businesses, but those who were unemployed became targets of a cruel new vagrancy law that empowered the police to act as on-the-spot judges. When a constable spied an unemployed black man, he was arrested, handcuffed and locked up in the local jail while more constables determined his sentence. There were three choices: sweep the (unpaved) streets, dig ditches or work on a chain gang. The constables decided the length of a man's sentence too. This new vagrancy law kept Las Vegas's population down, for it kept newcomers on the run from the police.

When the National Association for the Advancement of Colored People (NAACP) formed a branch in Las Vegas, many Westsiders joined, recognizing that black people needed to organize if they were to see laws enforced on their behalf. In 1939, the Nevada state legislature introduced a "Race and Color Bill" that would make it illegal to bar blacks from hotels, casinos and other public places. The NAACP took it one step further in Las Vegas, delivering a petition to the mayor and aldermen, stating: "all citizens or persons within the City of Las Vegas shall have equal enjoyment of accommodation advantages and privileges of all City property owned or leased by the City for public amusement, namely: City Parks, Golf Course, Cemetery, Swimming Pool and Library."

Casino owners lobbied against integration, claiming that admitting blacks would be bad for business. The petition was denied by the city, and the fair treatment legislation was dropped by the state Assembly. Although the 14th Amendment to the Constitution guarantees that no state may "deny any person life, liberty, or property," people of color in Nevada faced an uphill battle. Segregation in Las Vegas only got worse. The Hoover Dam became America's exciting new attraction, with over 300,000 visitors each year. To encourage more tourism, the city commissioners decided to redevelop and rezone the downtown area. Licenses were not renewed for businesses that didn't cater to tourists. Suddenly, places like Uncle Jake's Barbeque and Mammy Pinston's Plantation Kitchen were no longer welcome (though the bordellos could stay). Fremont Street was changing, and African-Americans were not part of the city's plan.

On the other side of the tracks, nothing changed. Over 200 people crowded into those 20 Westside blocks. The roads were still unpaved, and there was no sewer system. Decades earlier, J.T. McWilliams installed wells in the locations where the spring bubbled up. A tent near a Westside well rented for $5 a week. The best tents faced away from the roads, since every passing car stirred up a cloud of dust. When it rained, the hard red earth turned into one massive mud hole.

With the construction of an underpass in 1936, the Westside neighborhood finally became accessible. Commercial buildings were erected, then populated by black-owned businesses. A beauty parlor moved in, then a barbershop, bars, cafés and stores. When a movie theater was demolished in downtown Las Vegas, the theater's janitor hauled the bricks back to the Westside, where he built the neighborhood's first solid two-story structure. When the Las Vegas Water District brought in running water and built a sewer system, prospects for the Westside were looking better. The City even sent a truck to hose down the dusty roads twice a day.

As the facelift continued, a group of black men broached the idea of opening Westside casinos with city officials. These black entrepreneurs learned that it would be simple for them to acquire gaming and liquor licenses; to the Gaming Commission, Westside casinos promised to keep Fremont Street segregated.

Suddenly, Jackson Street became the Fremont Street of the Westside. Starting in 1945, new casinos opened with names like the Cotton Club,

El Morocco, the Brown Derby, the Elks Club and the New Town Tavern, all owned by black men. They hired black croupiers, security guards and restaurant staff, turning the Westside into a self-sustaining community.

Back on the east side of the tracks, black entertainers were prospering as well. Louis Armstrong, Pearl Bailey, Sammy Davis, Jr. and Nat King Cole were some of the biggest names at the most prominent clubs in whites-only Las Vegas. Despite their star billing, they were not permitted to stay in the hotels where they performed.

Those headliners found welcome instead at the Jackson Street casinos on the Westside, near their accommodations. On any night, it was not uncommon to see Cab Calloway, Billy Eckstine, Sammy Davis, Jr. and other black celebrities rolling dice and playing cards in the wee hours on Jackson Street.

The entertainment industry finally forced an end to segregation in Las Vegas. In November 1954, Sammy Davis, Jr., who was earning thousands each week at the Last Frontier, negotiated to stay in the V.I.P. suite and have access to the entire hotel, including its casino. Nat King Cole established a similar deal. Little fissures appeared in the once-impregnable "Whites Only" policy.

Then in May 1955 a new club opened on the Westside, the Moulin Rouge, the first integrated casino in the history of Las Vegas. Its success was immediate; a photo taken inside the Moulin Rouge appeared on the cover of *Life* magazine four weeks later. Business dropped east of the tracks as high rollers explored the integrated club. On May 26, 1960, with the participation of the NAACP, it was announced that segregation had ended in Las Vegas. The headline in the *Las Vegas Sun* read: "Businesses in Vegas Lift Color Barrier." It was official.

The NAACP assembled teams of 10 African-Americans to test the hotels' compliance. Each group reported the same successful experience:

they were welcomed at the door and welcomed at the tables. Fifty-five years after Las Vegas was founded, its black residents were finally allowed to gamble wherever they pleased.

The success of integration led to a rapid exodus on the Westside. With freedom to live anywhere, new arrivals weren't forced to seek refuge on the other side of the tracks any longer. Black entertainers and their entourages stayed at the hotels that hired them; now their contracts even stipulated the number of hours they needed to *remain* in the hotels after the show. The casinos on Jackson Street soon folded. Without the critical mass to keep their finances afloat, it was reported that sometimes a club owner would race to a pawnshop in the middle of the night to sell a ring or a watch because the club didn't have enough money to pay a big winner.

The neighborhood fell into disrepair. The Moulin Rouge suffered three fires in four years and was finally demolished in 2010. Churches have since replaced many of the shut-down casinos. Today, many of the lots that comprised the McWilliams Townsite are vacant land again.

N

2 The Cotton Club: 500 Jackson St.
5 Ebony Club: 501 West Jackson St.

Jackson Avenue

6 3 4

West Monroe Avenue

B Street

A Street

J Street
I Street
H Street
G Street
F Street
E Street
D Street
C Street

West Washington Avenue

578

East Washington Avenue

North Main Street
North 1st Street

Lions Memorial Park

North Las Vegas

McWilliams Townsite

Heritage Park

1

579

9

West Bonanza Road

15

East Bonanza Road

North Las Vegas Boulevard

93 95

West Ogden Avenue

East Stewart Avenue

515

West Sahara Avenue

602

Clark Townsite

East Sahara Avenue

West Sahara Avenue

7 10

589

Highland Drive

Circus Circus Drive

Las Vegas Boulevard South

171

Karen Avenue

Industrial Road

The Strip

Stardust Drive
East Desert Inn Road

East Desert Inn Road

8

Fashion Show Drive

Spring Mountain Road

Wynn Country Club

Sierra Vista Drive

1	McWilliams Townsite
2	The Cotton Club: 500 Jackson St.
3	El Morocco: 1322 North E. Street
4	The Brown Derby: 320 W. Monroe Ave.
5	Ebony Club: 501 West Jackson St.
6	Chick A Dee: 1314 North F Street
7	El Rancho: 2500 Las Vegas Blvd.
8	Sahara: 2535 Las Vegas Blvd. S.
9	Moulin Rouge: 900 West Bonanza Rd.
10	Last Frontier: 3120 Las Vegas Blvd. S.

■ Existing Building
■ Building No Longer Exists

250 ft
500 m

CHAPTER 15.

BREAKING THE COLOR BARRIER

Most visitors to Las Vegas didn't know that it was a segregated city until after they arrived. But what they found was referred to as the "Mississippi of the West." The barriers toppled slowly, with a little help from the city's powerful black entertainers.

JOSEPHINE BAKER

During her second performance at the Last Frontier in 1952, part of her American desegregation tour, Josephine Baker noticed that there were no black people in the audience. Between shows, she inquired about the hotel's policy regarding blacks in the showroom. "No Coloreds Allowed," she was told.

Baker's contract had stipulated that all of her shows be open to all, but management disagreed, claiming that her contract had been fulfilled the night before. If they did not permit blacks in for the second show, Baker promised to walk off the stage. From then on, as her contract demanded, she was guaranteed a table at each performance, which she reserved for members of the local NAACP.

← Josephine Baker, 1949

But there's another version of the story of Baker's show in Vegas with a more insidious twist. As the second performance approached, the hotel staff hovered near the showroom to witness the result. When the curtain went up, Baker looked out into the audience.

There in the front row was a black couple. The gentleman wore a tux and the lady was attired in an evening gown. It looked okay to Baker, so the show went on. The staff breathed a sigh of relief.

Only later was it discovered that the theater manager pulled a porter and a maid off their regular hotel shifts, dressed them in formalwear, planted them in the audience and told them to enjoy the show.

SAMMY DAVIS JR.

The Will Mastin Trio, featuring a young Sammy Davis, Jr., created a sensation as the opening act at the El Rancho.

Young Davis performed in song-and-dance routines with his father and "Uncle" Will Mastin, then he'd take the solo spotlight and make jaws drop. He was the first black entertainer to have the audacity to perform comic impressions of white celebrities. He was a howling success, delivering G-rated humor with an edge. The act was a spectacular hit on opening night.

But in 1945, where do you go to after opening night in Las Vegas when you're black?

As Davis already knew, the bar and casino at the El Rancho were for whites only, so there would be no celebration when the curtain came down. Parting company with his father and Will Mastin, he decided to catch a late-night movie by himself.

In the darkened theater, he walked down the aisle and sat in the front row. Suddenly he was yanked from his seat and dragged up the aisle and into the theater lobby. Stunned Sammy faced a sheriff's deputy in a big Western hat.

"What are you, boy, a wise guy?" He slapped Davis across the face. "Speak up when I talk to you."

Davis queried, "What'd I do?"

The deputy sneered, "Coloreds sit in the last three rows. You're in Nevada now, not New York. Mind our rules and you'll be treated square. Now go back and enjoy the movie, boy."

When the movie ended and the house lights came on, Davis saw that there were fewer than 10 people in the entire theater.

PEARL BAILEY
The Flamingo had been open for exactly four weeks when Pearl Bailey arrived.

Jimmy Durante opened the clubroom in its disastrous, inaugural two-week engagement. When the club re-opened two months later, Bugsy Siegel presented two weeks of Lena Horne. She was provided with accommodations at the Flamingo, the first person of color to stay at a resort on the Strip, but the casino was off-limits to her. Las Vegas was a segregated town, as some gentlemen with oil wells reminded the management. Amid his other headaches, Siegel had to make a public relations decision regarding people of color performing at the Flamingo.

In 1947, Bailey was a star on Broadway, in recordings and in Hollywood. She could now become a Las Vegas headliner too, at the invitation of Bugsy Siegel no less. But she'd have to stay on the dilapidated Westside.

In the confusion of the Flamingo's earliest days, when Bailey arrived at her dressing room backstage, she found her makeup table upended and the room in total disarray. She demanded to see the boss. To everyone's amazement, Siegel complied. He waited for his star backstage until she finished her act. Stepping offstage, Bailey nodded and kept walking.

Siegel followed Bailey to her dressing room. Observing the disarray, he took full responsibility. He pledged to take an inventory; he even promised a fresh tablecloth every night.

"Anything else?" he queried.

"I want a fire-engine-red Road Master Buick," Bailey is reported to have replied. "My car is in L.A. and taxis won't go to the Westside. I shouldn't be bumming a ride."

The next day, fresh tablecloths were stacked in her dressing room… and that night, in front of Mrs. Harrison's rooming house, a red Buick awaited, with keys in the ignition.

Nat King Cole, 1954

NAT KING COLE

Nat King Cole was an enormously popular crooner, earning $4,500 a week in Las Vegas in 1956. He headlined at the whites-only Thunderbird Hotel, where he wasn't allowed to venture beyond the showroom and the cook's resting area behind the kitchen. Cole's road manager was given a room in the hotel because he was white, but the high-paid feature attraction had to find other accommodations. He regularly stayed in a rooming house on the Westside.

Frank Sinatra was a great fan of Cole's. While performing at the Sands, Sinatra noticed that Cole almost always ate his dinner alone in his dressing room. Sinatra asked his valet, a black man named George, to find out why.

George explained the facts to Frank. "Coloreds aren't allowed in the dining room at the Sands."

Sinatra was enraged. He told the maître d' and the waitresses that if it ever happened again, he'd see that everyone was fired.

The next night, Sinatra invited Cole to dinner, making his guest the first black man to sit down and eat in the Garden Room at the Sands.

HARRY BELAFONTE

When Harry Belafonte performed in the showroom at the Sands, he was allowed to stay at the hotel, but the casino was off-limits. After his second show one night, at around 3 a.m., Belafonte tested the system.

Knowing that he wasn't supposed to be there, he stepped up to a blackjack table and put his cash on the felt-topped table. The dealer froze; he looked up to the surveillance camera overhead. Evidently, the bosses approved, since the dealer accepted Belafonte's money, gave him some chips, and the game was on.

Harry Belafonte, 1954

A crowd gathered to watch the handsome calypso singer, not particularly intrigued by the game, but simply to see what had once been unimaginable—the first black man to play cards on the Las Vegas Strip.

1   Last Frontier: 3120 Las Vegas Blvd. S.
2   El Rancho: 2500 Las Vegas Blvd.
3   Flamingo: 3555 Las Vegas Blvd. S.
4   The Sands: 3355 Las Vegas Blvd. S.
5   Thunderbolt Hotel: 2755 Las Vegas Blvd. S.

■ Existing Building
■ Building No Longer Exists

LIFE

LAS VEGAS—IS BOOM OVEREXTENDED?

THE WAR ON VIRUS DISEASES
ROBERT COUGHLAN TELLS OF SALK'S NEW GOALS

LAS VEGAS—IS BOOM OVEREXTENDED?

THE WAR ON VIRUS DISEASES
ROBERT COUGHLAN TELLS OF SALK'S NEW GOALS

NEWEST IN LAS VEGAS:
GIRLS AT THE MOULIN ROUGE

20 CENTS

JUNE 20, 1955

REG. U. S. PAT. OFF.

CHAPTER 16.

MOULIN ROUGE

They probably didn't know it at the time, but in 1944, the owners of the El Cortez on Fremont Street made history. They presented the Deep River Boys, the first black entertainers to perform at a white club in Las Vegas. The following year, Tip Tap Toe, a trio of African-American tap dancers filled the showroom in the Last Frontier for months.

Known to audiences for their one-reel movies, these dapper black men were a departure from the country-western acts that usually played in segregated Las Vegas. Black performers brought a different energy to Las Vegas stages, entertaining white patrons who kept on drinking and gambling. Club owners took notice.

On March 1, 1947, Lena Horne opened the nightclub at the Flamingo, the first luxury resort on the highway that would soon be called the Strip. She was the first in a succession of successful headliners, all of whom were black. From young Gregory Hines and his brother Maurice to the aging but exhilarating Nicholas Brothers, black performers found steady, high-profile work in Las Vegas.

← The Moulin Rouge on the cover of *Life* magazine, 1955

Of course, there was a catch. Las Vegas was a segregated town. Black performers, even high-paid headliners, weren't permitted to stay in the upscale hotels that were packed with their white fans. Instead, they were relegated to modest rooming houses on the dilapidated Westside. Every night, these performers ricocheted from adulation onstage to exclusion two shows later.

In the 1950s, the Las Vegas Strip underwent a real estate explosion. Eleven new resort hotels opened, ratcheting up the competition for big-name entertainers, accelerating the opportunities for African-American performers. Of equal importance: the first black-owned casinos opened on the ramshackle Westside. The clubs around Jackson Street launched a new era. Gaming licenses were easy to acquire, because, the logic went, African-American gamblers would stay out of clubs on the Strip if they had their own segregated casinos on the Westside.

It worked. For years, the Strip's celebrated black headliners, still heady from the ovations of their white audiences, took their business to the black-owned clubs on Jackson Street. Just about any night, black celebrities, their band members and crews could be found, in the wee hours past the second show, placing their bets on the Westside. Once again, club owners took notice.

The time had come to open an integrated club. In 1954, three white investors, entrepreneur Will Max Schwartz, restaurateur Louis Rubin and California real estate developer Alexander Bisno, joined forces. They teamed with the former boxing champion Joe Louis to open a new club at 900 West Bonanza Road, halfway between the black clubs on Jackson Street and the white world of Fremont Street. And they meant business.

At a cost of $3.5 million (that's over $28 million in 2010 dollars), the Moulin Rouge would be 11,000 square feet larger than the Flamingo. They intended to establish the Moulin Rouge as a real resort, not just another gambling den.

The Moulin Rouge opened on May 24, 1955, with the celebrated Joe Louis stationed at the front door to welcome guests. It was a triumph, hailed as the first integrated resort in Las Vegas. With hotel rooms and a restaurant, the Moulin Rouge was the ideal place for black entertainers to stay while performing on the white side of town, putting an end to the Westside's overpriced rooming houses. A mere four weeks later, a photo of the Moulin Rouge was featured on the cover of *Life* magazine, announcing the integrated hotel and casino to the entire nation.

Black artists who were banned from the casinos on the Strip found welcome at the Moulin Rouge, and so did their white friends and fans. Not only did top talent like Louis Armstrong, Pearl Bailey, Nat King Cole and Sammy Davis, Jr. perform in its showroom, but white performers including Frank Sinatra, George Burns, Liberace, Bob Hope and Jack Benny packed the place too. The Moulin Rouge even added a third show, at 2:30 a.m., to accommodate the excited crowds.

Success was palpable; the Westside was hot.

Stories conflict regarding what happened next, often based on conjecture. Officially, the Moulin Rouge owners declared bankruptcy after just six months of business, closing its doors in November 1955. The gangsters who controlled Las Vegas casinos in those days could not be pleased to see top performers attracting customers away from their Strip. Some said the Moulin Rouge couldn't pay its bills because the skimming was exorbitant; or, maybe the owners acquiesced to threats from rival club owners with mob ties. Regardless, the Moulin Rouge was no failure. Its rapid success served as the catalyst that ended segregation in Las Vegas.

In May 1960, when civil rights protestors threatened to march down the Las Vegas Strip to denounce Nevada's segregation enforcement, the doors to the Moulin Rouge were opened once more, for a meeting between black community leaders, Governor Grant Sawyer, NAACP President James McMillan, the Las Vegas mayor, and many hotel owners. Facilitated by Hank Greenspun, the publisher of the *Las Vegas Sun* newspaper, the participants finally agreed to end segregation in all of Las Vegas.

In 1992, the vacant Moulin Rouge building was declared a National Landmark for its key role in ending segregation. Although there were hopes that the casino might reopen, the Moulin Rouge suffered three fires in four years. The Neon Museum saved its historic neon sign, but the condemned building with the vibrant past was demolished in 2010.

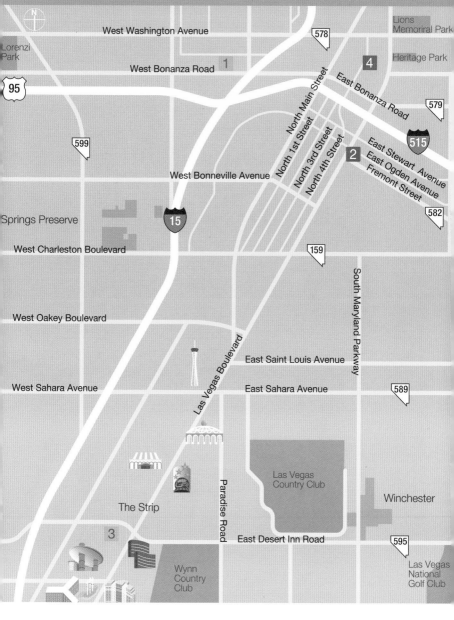

1   Moulin Rouge: 900 West Bonanza Road
2   El Cortez: 600 East Fremont Street
3   Last Frontier: 3120 Las Vegas Blvd S
4   Neon Museum: 821 Las Vegas Blvd. North

■ Existing Building
■ Building No Longer Exists

NEON MUSEUM AND NEON BONEYARD

Celebrate Las Vegas's glittering history at the Neon Museum, which has been preserving the city's unique signs—including the marquee from the Moulin Rouge—since 1996. Currently, the collection on display at the museum's Neon Boneyard displays 150 examples of this unique artform.

The Neon Museum offers Boneyard tours Tuesday through Saturday at 10 a.m. The minimum donation for our tours is $15.00 per person. Reservations are required and should be made at least two weeks in advance. For more information or to request a tour visit neonboneyard.org or call 702-387-NEON.

CHAPTER 17.

NAKED LADIES

With booze, cards and prostitutes in copious supply since Las Vegas's earliest days, even the town's toniest clubs felt like stag parties. It's no surprise; in the 1950s, when new clubs were opening on the Strip, the gamblers were nearly all men. Resorts paid top dollar to entertain them by presenting headliners direct from Hollywood or Broadway.

But in the 1950s, those resorts devised a new way to command top dollar from a predominantly male clientele: Put bare breasts onstage. Glorify (and exploit) the female anatomy in glitzy new revues. Burlesque was gasping its last breaths in rundown theaters across America, but you'd never know it in Las Vegas, where "exotic dancers" were the main attraction at some Strip hotels for decades. The city became famous for its spectacular girlie shows. Gentlemen in the audience were dazzled by sequins, feathers and flesh—though not necessarily in that order.

To merit the ticket price, the shows required a mystique. *Minsky's Follies*, the famous topless revue that scandalized New York in 1925, planned to shake up Las Vegas in 1957. Publicists crowed: How would Harold Minsky, the youngest brother, rejuvenate the *Follies* for a new

Burlesque comedian Tommy "Moe" Raft surrounded by showgirls

generation? Curiosity seekers saw for themselves at the Dunes Hotel on January 10, when *Minsky's Follies* exposed the first bare breasts in a Las Vegas showroom. The hit show ran for six years, unchanged.

Of course, bawdy girls were twirling their tassels on Block 16 for decades. Then came burlesque shows where ladies dropped their tops at the end of a song, just as the lights went out. Gypsy Rose Lee, Lili St. Cyr and other starlets performed stripteases like that, in upscale clubs like the El Rancho where nudity was taunted from behind a towel or an onstage bubble-bath. With banter from the stage, their acts were peppered with comedy and innuendo.

The finale of MGM Grand's *Crazy Horse Paris*

But this Minsky show was different: this was nudity with the lights on.

Decades earlier in New York, Minsky's could only present topless ladies
if they didn't move. Now in Las Vegas, his massive production numbers
featured glamorous, long-legged ladies baring their breasts while
strutting down staircases in expensive costumes made of rhinestones and
beads. The tassel-twirlers on Block 16 were raucous fun for a generation
of cowboys, but to these postwar gentlemen, *Minsky's Follies* was art.

Part of *Minsky's* success came from simply being first. Competitors
needed a different angle, and they found it in the cabarets of Paris. The
Lido de Paris opened at the Stardust on July 2, 1958, a feature that

continued until 1992. On December 24, 1959, the *Folies Bergère* opened at the Tropicana, where it played for 49 consecutive years.

Productions became more elaborate. For the *Lido de Paris* show, the Stardust's showroom was outfitted with hydraulic stage lifts, an 11-by-30-foot swimming pool and an ice rink that could be brought to the stage level in 15 seconds. Topless girls lined the revolving stage "like a living curtain," according to a *Las Vegas Sun* columnist. Others leaped from platforms into the onstage pool.

The revues offered what Las Vegas lacked: Spectacle. Before *Minsky's* arrived, performers fit one of three categories. There was music, from the Gumm Sisters at the Meadows to Lena Horne at the Flamingo. There was comedy, from Milton Berle to Jerry Lewis to Don Rickles. And there was dance, from the senior Nicholas Brothers to young Sammy Davis Jr. in the Will Mastin Trio. In all cases, famous or not, the performer was the star. Now came revues where the production was the star. The appeal of these spectacles ratcheted up the production values for performers everywhere on the Strip. Sinatra's band got bigger, Liberace's costumes got gaudier, and for his comeback, even Elvis Presley wore rhinestones.

Business has been steady ever since. New versions of *Minsky's Follies* appeared in Las Vegas landmarks like the Silver Slipper, the Thunderbird and the Aladdin. The Stardust added variations, rotating its *Lido* show with the *Mambo Showgirls of Havana* and the *Carnival Women of Brazil,* among others. Those hotels are gone, but new spectacles continue to thrive, like *Crazy Horse Paris* at the MGM Grand, *Jubilee* at Bally's and the *Crazy Girls* at the Riviera.

The only difference between then and now? You can buy your tickets online.

M

North Las Vegas Airport

North Las Vegas

Petitti Park

East Lake Mead Boulevard

147

599

15

West Owens Avenue

Hartke Park

East Owens Avenue

Las Vegas Golf Club

578

West Washington Avenue

North Main Street
North 1st Street
North 3rd Streets
North 4th Streets

Lions Memoriral Park

East Washington Avenue

Freedom Park

Lorenzi Park

95

West Bonanza Road

Heritage Park

579

East Bonanza Road

3

Nature Park

West Bonneville Avenue

East Stewart Avenue
East Ogden Avenue
Fremont Street

515

Hadland Park

Springs Preserve

West Charleston Boulevard

159

Las Vegas Boulevard

East Charleston Boulevard

582

West Sahara Avenue

2

East Sahara Avenue

589

Jaycee Park

5

8

Las Vegas Country Club

South Valley View Boulevard

12
11

4

7

Paradise Road

East Desert Inn Road

Winchester

595

Winchester Community Center

Wynn Country Club

Sands Avenue

Las Vegas National Golf Club

The Strip

6

East Flamingo Road

1

9
10

East Harmon Avenue

East Tropicana Avenue

East Reno Avenue

McCarran International Airport

LAS VEGAS

1 mile
1 km

Emerald Green Course

1	The Dunes: 3600 Las Vegas Blvd. S.
2	El Rancho: 2500 Las Vegas Blvd.
3	Block 16: FIrst through Second streets, from Stewart to Ogden avenues
4	Stardust: 3000 Las Vegas Blvd. S.
5	Meadows: Fremont Street and Boulder Highway
6	Flamingo: 3555 Las Vegas Blvd. S.
7	Silver Slipper: 3100 Las Vegas Blvd. S.
8	Thunderbird: 2755 Las Vegas Blvd. S.
9	Aladdin: 3667 Las Vegas Blvd. S.
10	MGM Grand: 3799 Las Vegas Blvd. S.
11	Bally's 3645 Las Vegas Blvd. S.
12	Riviera: 2901 Las Vegas Blvd. S.

■ Existing Building
■ Building No Longer Exists

CHAPTER 18.

THE SKIM

Quickly defined: The Skim was the process of removing cash from the day's proceeds before those proceeds were totaled up and recorded on the books.

No taxes were paid on the unreported gains. The skim was cash that was never recorded; it just disappeared. Daily.

In every casino, there's a Hard Count Room, a secure site under continual surveillance by cameras where the money is counted. Periodically, the drop box under each gaming table is retrieved by security guards who take the cash to the Hard Count Room. The cash accumulates until the next day, when its contents are officially counted and the day's take is entered on the books. The proceeds from slot machines are retrieved this way too, although the coins are often weighed rather than counted.

The Skim worked very simply: mobsters who ran the casinos had their operatives in the Hard Count Room when the money was counted. During the count, some wise guy would walk in with a box or a bag,

stuff it with cash and then walk out. Of course, nobody saw anything. According to one FBI confession, there are "21 holes in the bucket," meaning there are an estimated 21 methods for skimming, even while under camera surveillance in the counting room. In addition to the bagmen, there were other obvious ruses, like shielding the "eye in the sky" camera over every table at a key moment when the drop box was being collected.

With all the money pouring into Vegas casinos, this untaxed money was used to repay investors, not the IRS. Owners concealed much of their income from the late 1940s until Attorney General Robert F. Kennedy arrived in the 1960s. To the Mob, the Skim was decades of pure profit.

Susan Berman, daughter of gangster David Berman, once recalled her visits to the Hard Count Room with her father, where they watched the money being separated into ones, fives, tens and hundreds: "I saw them go – 'three for us, one for the government, two for Meyer [Lansky].' I helped them count the bills. The skimming, of course, it was a crime. But it wasn't a crime like having to kill people."

As sleek, new hotels sprang up along the Strip, the Skim was institutionalized in comfortable new surroundings. When the Gaming Control Board raided the Stardust, for example, they discovered a secret vault constructed in the hotel, just for the Skim, packed with bags and bags of coins that had been systematically diverted from the slot machines. The owners had even set up a fake weighing machine to conceal how much they were skimming.

Dennis Gomes, then head of the audit division for the Control Board learned first-hand of the dangers of intervening with the Skim. "I got a gun in the stomach when we broke up the Stardust scam," he reported.

There was another trick to the Skim. It was always difficult and sometimes impossible for authorities to determine the actual owners of

---

← Frank Costello testifies before the Kefauver Committee investigating organized crime, 1951

the casinos, as long as the staff in the Hard Count Room maintained its poker face. The Nevada Gaming Commission did its background checks and awarded licenses to individuals, but they were frequently foils for bigger racketeers who would never have passed Nevada's scrutiny if they'd been the applicants for the gaming license.

One of the most celebrated absentee cases involved Frank Costello, considered to be one of the most ruthless thugs in America. (Hollywood insiders claim that Marlon Brando based his characterization of Don Corleone in *The Godfather* on the voice of Frank Costello.) Although Senator Estes Kefauver put Costello through a grueling investigation in 1951, the most that Kefauver could pin on Costello was a contempt charge, for which he received an 18-month sentence.

Years later, on the evening of May 2, 1957, a gunman waited in the foyer of The Majestic, a fashionable apartment house where millionaire Costello made his home in New York City. When Costello arrived, the gunman shouted: "This is for you Frank!" before gunning down Costello in the elegant lobby and escaping in a waiting car.

Costello was rushed to a nearby hospital. As doctors removed a .38 slug from behind his ear, detectives searched through the pockets of his jacket and pants. What they found was a revelation: a slip of paper with some handwritten notes: "Gross casino wins as of 4/27/57, $657,284; Casino wins less markers, $434,695; slot wins $62,844; Markers 153,745."

Costello, whose criminal record would have prevented him from owning a Las Vegas casino, owned one anyway! He was carrying handwritten details about a casino that was enormously profitable. ($657,000 in 1957 equals about $5 million today.) Detectives at the Nevada Gaming Control Board soon discovered that the $657,284 figure matched the gross receipts for the brand new Tropicana Hotel during its first 24 days of operation. That's how much the Tropicana *reported*.

Costello's concealed ownership of the Tropicana might have remained a secret for years. Once it was revealed, he and his associates were ordered to sell their interests in Las Vegas.

1 Stardust: 3000 Las Vegas Blvd. S.
2 Fremont Hotel: 200 Fremont St.
3 Tropicana: 3801 Las Vegas Blvd. S.

■ Existing Building
▨ Building No Longer Exists

CHAPTER 19.

BOBBY, JIMMY AND MOE

Moe Dalitz had *chutzpah*. Only in Las Vegas could a notorious Jewish bootlegger be hailed as the town's greatest philanthropist.

Dalitz made his fortune during Prohibition, controlling bootleg liquor in Cleveland. Like Meyer Lansky in New York, Dalitz formed strong ties with the Italian-American underworld. When Prohibition ended, he changed his business to illegal casinos in Ohio and Kentucky.

In the 1940s, stuffy American bankers wouldn't lend construction funds to risky projects like Las Vegas casinos. So Dalitz merged his operation with Lansky's Syndicate to satisfy the growing demand; organized crime became the primary source for development funds on the Las Vegas Strip.

Just as Lansky's money bailed out the Flamingo, a similar story unfolded down the street, where entrepreneur Wilbur Clark ran out of money halfway through construction of the Desert Inn. This time, it was Dalitz who had the cash to complete the construction. Wilbur Clark's Desert Inn opened on April 24, 1950, though Clark was the owner in name only; he

Moe Dalitz, Elvis Presley, Juliet Prowse, Wilbur and Toni Clark, Cecil Simmons

had given up 75 percent of the operation to Dalitz. Of the five resorts on the Strip, the Desert Inn was the only one with a real 18-hole golf course. It was an immediate success; the first week's profits were reportedly in excess of $750,000 (nearly $7 million today).

A chef from the Ritz Hotel in Paris was recruited to oversee the Gourmet Room and ventriloquist Edgar Bergen headlined on opening night in the luxurious, 450-seat Painted Desert Room. In the decades that followed, this intimate space became one of the most celebrated nightclubs in America: the site of Frank Sinatra's first gig on the Las Vegas Strip and home to shows by entertainers including Bobby Darin, Tony Bennett, Wayne Newton, Cher, Jerry Lewis, Don Rickles and Tina Turner. To Dalitz, however, the most important name at the casino was Allard Rosen, imported from Cleveland to manage the casino. A successful night at the Desert Inn meant a bountiful skim for Dalitz and company.

After years of running illegal gambling operations in Ohio, Dalitz and his cronies had the expertise to run a casino. They knew how to spot the wise guys who would try to beat them at the tables or in the counting rooms, and they knew how to deal with them when they were caught. As actress and former hotel owner Debbie Reynolds put it: "No one got killed that wasn't supposed to."

Dalitz reveled in the irony that without changing professions, a Cleveland criminal had become an upstanding citizen in Las Vegas. He took an interest in civic affairs, raised funds to build the Sunrise Hospital, supported the Las Vegas Public Library and contributed thousands to local charities. Unlike Lansky, who shunned the spotlight, Dalitz spearheaded so many city projects that by 1960, the former bootlegger was hailed as "Mr. Las Vegas."

That year was significant for Las Vegas. Fidel Castro's revolution had just shuttered all of Havana's famous casinos. In September, United Airlines introduced nonstop jetliner service to Vegas, slashing travel time from the East Coast in half. Las Vegas was more appealing than ever.

Dalitz saw the opportunity: the city was about to face its biggest boom yet. To meet the demand, the Desert Inn needed more hotel rooms. Lots of them. But for that, he needed cash.

That's when Mr. Las Vegas grasped a harsh reality: Las Vegas was about to experience enormous growth, but organized crime didn't have pockets deep enough to make it expand the way they wanted it to expand. The skim at the Desert Inn just wasn't big enough to pay for the kind of expansion the hotel merited. Dalitz needed to find another investor, someone with access to even greater funds. He knew just whom to call.

Jimmy Hoffa, president of the Teamsters Union, was called all kinds of things, and they were rarely flattering. So when he received the call from his old friend Moe Dalitz, he fancied a new title: Portfolio Manager.

By 1960, The International Brotherhood of Teamsters was growing at an exponential rate. Originally a confluence of Midwest truck drivers and warehouse workers, the labor union reached 75,000 members in 1933. By 1952, when Hoffa was national vice president, the Teamsters had grown to over a million members, and by 1957, when Hoffa was elected president, membership exceeded 1.5 million.

In 1955, most truck drivers in America had no pensions, unlike workers in steel mills and auto plants. In new contracts, Hoffa bargained with trucking employers, securing pension payments of $2 per worker per week. That payment had been ratcheted up to $4 weekly by 1960 when Dalitz came calling. The Teamsters pension fund was collecting $5 million a month, with very few legal strictures as to how the cash could be invested. To casino owners in Las Vegas, it appeared that Hoffa was sitting on one spectacular pot of gold.

Hoffa took an aggressive, if speculative, approach to investing. The primary goal of the Teamsters' new loan policy would be, as he put it, "to reward friends and to make new ones." With that blessing, the Desert Inn acquired a nine-story addition just in time to accommodate the surge in Las Vegas tourism. The relationship between Dalitz and Hoffa had changed the Las Vegas skyline. And everybody's skim got bigger.

To the owners on the Strip, Hoffa was a hero. They were used to hustling the IRS, illegally underreporting their casinos' productivity, but Hoffa's

Wilbur Clark stands in front of his Desert Inn

source of revenue was clean and legal. He had negotiated a deal on behalf of the union, then watched the money pour in. Now it was time to "reward friends." It wasn't Hoffa's money, and a sizable chunk went to pensioners every month. But the return on investment remained steady.

As the nonstop flights arrived in Las Vegas in the early 1960s, millions of dollars from the Teamsters pension fund were invested in the city, building or expanding landmarks like Caesars Palace, Circus Circus, the Sands, the Dunes, the Stardust, plus the Castaways in Miami and the Eastgate Coliseum and Cleveland Raceways in Ohio. In his new role as Portfolio Manager, Hoffa charged 6.5 percent interest annually and made no apologies. To his critics within the union, he asked: "What other large industry pays a pension of close to $200 every month?" He had a point.

Attorney General Robert F. Kennedy also had a point to make. He felt that unions should be protecting people, not exploiting their pensions in gambling dens.

From 1957 to 1960 Robert F. Kennedy served as chief counsel for John L. McClellan's Senate hearings, officially titled the United States Senate Select Committee on Improper Activities in Labor and Management. The Committee issued its first report on March 24, 1958, condemning Hoffa and accusing the union leader of gathering enough power to destroy the national economy.

In televised hearings watched by 1.2 million American households, the Committee detailed the Teamsters' misuse of union funds, its ties to labor racketeers and organized crime. It was intended to expose the corruption of the Hoffa regime, but at the last minute, a number of witnesses recanted their written testimony and the hearings fizzled. The Senate couldn't catch Hoffa.

Three years later, the Vegas deal with Dalitz led the new Attorney General right back to Hoffa. Kennedy vowed to collar those who had eluded the government, informing his staff: "Organized crime syndicates have become an insidious rot, infesting the nation's innermost core." Jimmy Hoffa was at the top of Kennedy's list.

Over the next two years, the Justice Department, the FBI and the IRS waged an all-out war on Las Vegas, planting illegal wiretaps, plotting raids and scrutinizing the financial records of every casino in town. In 1963, they succeeded where other investigations had failed. Kennedy publicly exposed the Skim.

It was a public relations disaster for Las Vegas. Newspapers, radios and televisions nationwide brayed that mobsters were pilfering an estimated $10 million annually from Vegas casinos. An exposé called *The Green Felt Jungle* became an immediate bestseller. The Justice Department handed out indictments everywhere, hauling in 600 organized crime figures in 1963 alone.

Hoffa was convicted of multiple offenses. The government finally caught him on a witness tampering charge in 1964 when a Teamsters insider provided key testimony, and he was convicted of misappropriating union funds later that year. After exhausting his appeals, Hoffa went to prison in 1967.

Dalitz faced indictments for tax evasion. Residents realized that Las Vegas would now be subject to relentless government scrutiny. Alliances with mobsters had become a liability. "Mr. Las Vegas" stepped out of the spotlight.

In 1976, Dalitz was named Humanitarian of the Year by the American Cancer Research Center and Hospital. In 1982 he received the Torch of Liberty Award from the Anti-Defamation League. When he died of natural causes in 1989, many organizations received substantial donations that he left for them in his will. The ex-bootlegger proved his title as the city's biggest philanthropist.

On October 23, 2001, the Desert Inn was demolished. It's now the site of the Wynn Las Vegas, another resort with its own golf course.

1 The Flamingo: 3555 Las Vegas Blvd. S.
2 Desert Inn: 3145 Las Vegas Blvd. S.
3 Sunrise Hospital: 3186 South Maryland Parkway
4 Las Vegas Public Library: 833 Las Vegas Blvd. N.
5 Caesar's Palace: 3570 Las Vegas Blvd. S.
6 Circus Circus: 2880 Las Vegas Blvd. S.
7 The Sands: 3355 Las Vegas Blvd. S.
8 The Dunes: 3600 Las Vegas Blvd. S.
9 The Stardust: 3000 Las Vegas Blvd. S.
10 Wynn Las Vegas: 3131 Las Vegas Blvd. S.

■ Existing Building
■ Building No Longer Exists

CHAPTER 20.

THE RAT PACK

With jets arriving nonstop every day, star power on the Strip every night and atomic bomb explosions on schedule, Las Vegas was mighty intriguing in 1960. Warner Brothers decided to cash in on that intrigue, giving a greenlight to *Ocean's Eleven*, a caper about five simultaneous casino heists on New Year's Eve. They planned to film on location too, featuring the three biggest headliners in Las Vegas: Frank Sinatra, Dean Martin and Sammy Davis, Jr. Rounding out the cast were comedian Joey Bishop and Hollywood heartthrob Peter Lawford, who was in the papers for a different reason. His wife was Patricia Kennedy, sister of Senator John Kennedy, now a presidential candidate. Sinatra referred to him as "Brother-in-Lawford."

The Sands was the swankiest resort on the Strip and was prominently featured in the movie. When Judy Garland headlined at its Copa Room, she invited two audience members to the stage: Frank Sinatra and Dean Martin. The audience enjoyed it so much that the guys didn't leave the stage for 20 minutes. The camaraderie between these two Italian-American stars was such a crowd-pleaser that the Sands management sought to make them an attraction. With *Ocean's Eleven* in town, they

← The Rat Pack at the Sands: Frank Sinatra, Dean Martin, Sammy Davis, Jr., Peter Lawford and Joey Bishop, 1960

The Tremendous Trio: Dean Martin, Sammy Davis, Jr., and Frank
Sinatra, 1961

succeeded. From January 20 to February 16, 1960, all five film stars
would appear in the luxurious Copa Room at the Sands, when shooting
on *Ocean's Eleven* wrapped for the day.

The show was billed as "The Summit at the Sands," a nod to the Paris
Summit where the U.S. and Russia had recently faced off. But the
moniker didn't stick. The press and the hardcore fans resurrected the
"Rat Pack," a title that Sinatra thought he had left behind in L.A.

Casino magnate Steve Wynn was there to witness the magic. "The air
in the Sands crackled. The electricity in the building that afternoon
was beyond belief. There is no parallel to it today," he recalled. "The
lights go out. The band plays the music, and an announcer's voice says,
'Welcome to the Sands's Copa Room.' And then without another word,

the curtain opens and Frank Sinatra walks out, with no introduction."

The audience went wild, expecting a lower-billed name to come first. Sinatra sang six songs, then introduced Joey Bishop, and the onstage party commenced. Witnesses call it Las Vegas's golden moment. Every hotel room was booked at top rates; tables in the casinos were packed. The Sands raked in a fortune.

It was a demanding schedule: the Rat Pack did two shows each night, followed by an extended stretch of boozing in the lounge in the pre-dawn hours while the film crews set up the next day's shoot.

At daybreak, the men recovered in the Sands's steam room, where they'd pull themselves together. The VIPs who were permitted in the spa afterhours had white bathrobes with their nicknames embroidered on them (except for Sammy Davis. His was brown). Sinatra was nicknamed "The Pope," Davis was "Smokey" and Martin was "Dago." They'd sober up, get a massage, then fall asleep in the spa.

The show was more than just famous singers crooning the great American songbook; it had an edge. It was the era when nobody brought kids to Sin City. These guys were swingers: bad boys who earned their moniker as the Rat Pack, laughing and boozing it up onstage while cheating on their wives and mingling with the Mob when they weren't filming a movie. Sinatra was even a partner; he owned 7 percent of the Sands's casino. These high-wire lives on public display were topped by private lives among the city's infamous bimbos and alleged gangsters — and the Skim.

Those clamoring for tickets to see the Rat Pack included jet-setting socialites, Hollywood insiders and even politicians. Campaigning for President, Senator John F. Kennedy met with Nevada delegates in Las Vegas on February 7, 1960; then it was time to see his brother-in-law cavort with Sinatra and friends onstage at the Sands.

WHY A "RAT PACK?"

In 1955, when a gang of hoodlums clashed with the Los Angeles police, local newspapers referred to the young perps as a "rat pack."

On the other side of town, actor Humphrey Bogart hosted a dinner party. When the guests assembled, Bogart's wife, Lauren Bacall, joked: "I see the rat pack is all here." The guests were amused, since they could hardly be confused with the bad boys on the wrong side of the law.

However, the next day, columnist Joe Hyams turned it into news in the *New York Herald Tribune*: "The Rat Pack held its first annual meeting last night at Romanoff's restaurant in Beverly Hills and elected officers for the coming year. Named to executive positions were: Frank Sinatra, pack master; Judy Garland, first vice president; Lauren Bacall, den mother; Sid Luft, cage master; Humphrey Bogart, rat in charge of public relations." An institution was born.

It didn't hang together for very long. Bogart died of cancer less than two years later; Bacall moved to New York; Luft and Garland divorced. That left Sinatra with a title he didn't need. Already a juicy source of Hollywood gossip for his hot temper, his tempestuous marriage to Ava Gardner (and his alleged suicide attempt when the love affair soured), his ebbing music career, his Oscar for *From Here to Eternity*—Sinatra's ups and downs garnered all the attention a performer could want. He didn't need to perpetuate this one-night gag at Romanoff's.

In Las Vegas five years later, when the *Ocean's Eleven* cast performed to great acclaim at the Sands, enough fans and pundits recalled the Rat Pack moniker to make it stick. Peter Lawford, Joey Bishop, Dean Martin, Sammy Davis, Jr. and Frank Sinatra are now remembered as the official Rat Pack, a term they avoided.

When John F. Kennedy ran for president in 1960, the five stars campaigned for him, all the way to the Democratic National Convention in Los Angeles. Sinatra was so supportive of the candidate that he spontaneously renamed the entertainers "the Jack Pack," the closest he ever came to acknowledging the Rat Pack label.

Davis described that first night with JFK in his autobiography: "We always had celebrities in the audience. All five of us were onstage and we'd introduce them round-robin, each of us taking one, always saving the biggest for last. That night, Frank stepped back to where we had a bar on the stage and as I was pouring a drink he said, 'Smokey, you introduce the President.' Frank threw that to me!" Davis did the honors, introducing Senator Kennedy to the audience at the Sands.

JFK partied with the cast after the show, when Sinatra fixed him up with voluptuous Judy Campbell. Their affair went on for years. It was even alleged that Campbell was the Mob courier who delivered vast amounts of cash to JFK's campaign. (That allegation put FBI chief J. Edgar Hoover on the case. The illicit affair with Campbell ended in 1962, while Kennedy was America's 35th president.) That same night, Lawford whispered to Davis that the Strip owners had made a huge contribution to Jack's campaign. "If you want to see what a million dollars in cash looks like, go into the next room; there's a brown leather satchel in the closet." But as Davis confessed in his book: "I got out of there. Some things you don't want to know."

The Rat Pack "summits" continued more informally at the Sands after filming wrapped on *Ocean's Eleven*. While the film did just adequate business for Warner Brothers, the combination of personalities encouraged the studio to develop more material for the Rat Pack. In June 1961, they reteamed for the film *Sergeants 3* with principal photography in nearby Utah, and commuted to Vegas at night. Martin celebrated his 44th birthday during that engagement, an event so special that United Press International reported more than 2,000 people were turned away. The over-capacity crowd was lined two-deep along the Copa's walls, along with friends at ringside including Elizabeth Taylor, Eddie Fisher, Marilyn Monroe and Andy Williams. As UPI reported, the headliners wheeled out a five-foot-tall birthday cake in the shape of a J&B Scotch bottle. Martin threw the first piece of cake at Davis, Davis fired back, and

Frank Sinatra and Patrice Wymore in *Ocean's 11*, 1960

the whole event devolved into a massive food fight at the Copa.

"Drop in" shows became semi-regular affairs at the Sands, where the marquee would tease: "Dean Martin, Maybe Frank, Maybe Sammy." Their onstage antics soared. If something funny occurred spontaneously, it stayed in the act; Joey Bishop wrote the other "ad-libs." In one outrageous gag, Martin held up the impish Davis and announced, "I'd like to thank the NAACP for this award." The crowd roared at every performance.

Politics eventually broke up the "Jack Pack," and its members began to unravel. They had all campaigned for Kennedy, even appearing together at the Democratic National Convention in July 1960. But in 1963, with Kennedy in the White House, Lawford asked Sinatra for a favor: Would he host the President as a guest at his Palm Springs house? Sinatra was honored; he went to great lengths, even constructing a helipad to accommodate the President's arrival. However, Attorney General Robert F. Kennedy, on a crusade against organized crime, advised the President to avoid socializing with Sinatra because of his association with Las Vegas mobsters. The President's visit was canceled; Kennedy stayed at Bing Crosby's estate instead. Sinatra was incensed; he blamed Lawford for this snub and banished him from the team. In an especially spiteful move, Lawford's role in the film *Robin and the 7 Hoods* was given to Bing Crosby instead. Sinatra later abandoned the Democratic Party.

Sinatra was notorious for keeping his winnings and ignoring his gambling losses, but these infractions were forgiven by the mobsters who ran the Sands, who appreciated the business he attracted. Then in 1967, the Sands was purchased by Ava Gardner's former beau Howard Hughes. With Hughes's Mormon Mafia in charge, Sinatra could not exceed a $200,000 line of credit. On September 11, 1967, when pit boss Carl Cohen informed Sinatra that he had reached his credit limit, the enraged Sinatra threw a fistful of chips in Cohen's face. Cohen decked him, knocking out Sinatra's two front teeth. The headline in the next day's *Las Vegas Sun* screamed "Sinatra Loses Teeth in Strip Hotel Brawl." The incident made national news and ended Sinatra's long-term association with the Sands. The next day, press releases from Caesars Palace proclaimed the coming of "the noblest Roman of them all." Sinatra moved his act to the 1,100-seat Circus Maximus showroom, nearly double the size of the Copa. He never returned to the Sands.

Martin quit the Sands too, and found a string of successes: a network television show and a prolific career in films. He inaugurated the Celebrity Room at the brand new MGM Grand in December 1973 and packed the place steadily for years.

The group reunited, to Sinatra's delight, on the opening night of engagement at Bally's on October 29, 1987. During the show, Davis entered from stage left and Martin entered from stage right. But the humor and the timing felt forced; the dynamic had changed. It was the last time the three headliners stood together onstage in Las Vegas.

Lawford's career faded after his banishment from the Rat Pack. He divorced Pat Kennedy in 1966, then remarried three times, each time to women who were decades younger. (The last was 17.) Alcohol and drug abuse reduced his work to sporadic guest appearances on television. He died from cirrhosis of the liver and kidney failure at age 61.

Davis died of throat cancer in 1990. He was buried with a gold watch given to him by Sinatra. On May 18, 1990, two days after his death, the lights on the Strip were dimmed for 10 minutes in tribute to his many accomplishments in Las Vegas.

The lights on the Strip were dimmed again, in 1995, when Martin died at age 78.

In 1997, Frank Sinatra was inducted into the Gaming Hall of Fame. The recipient of endless awards, including a Doctorate from the University of Nevada at Las Vegas for his generous fundraising on their behalf, Sinatra died in Beverly Hills in 1998 at age 82. Joey Bishop was the only surviving Rat Pack member to attend his funeral. On May 15, 1998, the lights on the Las Vegas Strip were dimmed once again in a final 10-minute tribute.

Bishop lived longest. Following the breakup of the Rat Pack, he starred in television shows twice, though neither became a long-running hit. He died of heart failure at his home in California in October 2007, 15 weeks shy of his 90th birthday.

The Sands, the seventh major resort to be built on the Strip, was demolished in 1996. Two very different Italian-Americans occupy the site today. Though Frank and Dean are gone, it's now site of the Venetian and Palazzo hotels.

1 The Sands: 3355 Las Vegas Blvd. S.
2 Caesar's Palace: 3570 Las Vegas Blvd. S.
3 MGM Grand: 3645 Las Vegas Blvd. S.
4 Bally's: 3645 Las Vegas Blvd. S.
5 The Venetian: 3355 Las Vegas Blvd. S.
6 The Palazzo: 3325 Las Vegas Blvd. S.
7 UNLV Center for Gaming Research/
   Gaming Hall of Fame: 987 E. Harmon Ave.

■ Existing Building
□ Building No Longer Exists

CHAPTER 21.

THE SWEET SCIENCE

Could there be a better place for boxing to flourish than in Las Vegas? Since its founding, the population was overwhelmingly male. For decades, the town catered to male pleasures: hookers were legal, bootleggers didn't get caught, gamblers packed the casinos, and girls onstage were topless. Add to that regularly scheduled spectacles, as Las Vegas eventually hosted some of the world's most memorable title fights.

Boxers start with a blank canvas. There is little equipment required, there aren't many rules, and there are no teams to organize. The sweet science is a face-off between two opposing forces, a metaphor for life's competitions. It can be subtle too: immigrant vs. native son, loud vs. humble, intellectual vs. brute, you name it. Two individuals locked in bloody combat; it's been part of the human experience since the day holy Cain slew Abel.

The first fight in Nevada is famous. In the 1800s, prizefighting was against the law in all 45 states until January 1897, when the rogue state of Nevada was the first to legalize prizefights. In March, at the Carson City racetrack, "Gentleman Jim" Corbett defended his heavyweight title

← Muhammad Ali stands over a fallen Sonny Liston in Las Vegas, 1965

The Corbett-Fitzsimmons fight, March 17, 1897

against British Bob Fitzsimmons, competing for a $25,000 purse. Movie cameras had just been invented. This match, the first legal prizefight in America, was filmed with one of the very first silent movie cameras. *The Corbett-Fitzsimmons Fight* was the longest film ever made at that time. And it promptly triggered the first censorship law against the film industry: Since prizefights were illegal in all other states, then movies of prizefights must be illegal there too. (In an ironic twist, when Corbett lost the championship fight, he became an actor in silent movies.)

As soon as other states legalized prizefighting, Nevada's popularity plummeted. Overriding the governor's veto, the legislature imposed the Jim Crow laws of the day. Nevada's boxing statute decreed that both boxers had to be white men. This caveat sidelined Las Vegas from boxing's mainstream for decades. Race relations were played out in the ring for much of the 20th century, but not in Las Vegas, where "athletic contests" were local events. Title fights never came to Las Vegas.

Television changed the paradigm. The boxing ring fit nicely on the first black-and-white television screens; it was easy to follow two dueling opponents. The sweet science dominated early television; boxing was on almost every night of the week. And it was popular: fight nights regularly attracted over 30 percent of the primetime audience. Boxing even sold televisions. Arenas with the technology to broadcast the fights were the most appealing venues now.

When boxing was televised from Las Vegas for the first time on May 27, 1960, prizefighters found a new welcome in Nevada. The 15-round welterweight championship at the Convention Center signaled the city's entry into high profile televised matches. New resorts going up on the Strip included arenas with over 15,000 seats, plus state-of-the-art set-ups for television equipment.

Las Vegas elevated boxing into a spectacle. More than a contest, a fight became an event. While hosting some of the most memorable title fights in history, a well-polished industry of lights, limos, promoters and media ratcheted up the excitement. It continues today: prizefighters battle for multi-million-dollar purses, tickets sell for jaw-dropping figures, and ever-greater fortunes are wagered in the sports betting rooms. Title fights in Las Vegas even make national news.

TOP DOLLAR

Las Vegas continues to top its own financial records in the arena, attracting some of the largest crowds and generating some of the richest gates in boxing history.

The title fight between Larry Holmes and Gerry Cooney on June 11, 1982 at Caesars Palace drew 29,214 people, breaking every indoor attendance record in North American history. At the time, it was the biggest closed-circuit/pay-per-view production ever, broadcast to over 150 countries.

The "Fight of the Millennium" between Oscar De La Hoya and Felix "Tito" Trinidad, Jr. set the record for highest-grossing non-heavyweight fight: $12,949,500. On September 18, 1999, at the Mandalay Bay Resort and Casino, the fight topping the record for most-watched pay-per-view customers, with almost 1.5 million buys.

That event was topped by the heavyweight bout between Evander Holyfield and Lennox Lewis on November 13, 1999, at the Thomas & Mack Center at the University of Nevada at Las Vegas, which generated approximately $16,860,300; figures vary according to sources.

The self-proclaimed Pay-Per-View King, Floyd Mayweather, Jr., claimed his title in 2007 with a highly publicized fight against. Oscar De La Hoya at the MGM Grand. Setting, another record for the highest grossing boxing gate, the welterweight fight sold out in three hours, generating ticket sales that grossed $18,419,200, with an additional 2.15 million Pay Per View buys; De La Hoya alone made $52 million, though he lost the fight. Mayweather remained undefeated, both in the ring, and in proceeds.

Floyd Patterson vs. Sonny Liston, Las Vegas Convention Center
July 22, 1963

The first heavyweight championship fight in Las Vegas was a grudge match.

Floyd Patterson, the popular heavyweight champ, was also a soft-spoken hero to the African-American community during years of civil rights struggles. Challenger Sonny Liston was an ex-convict with reputed mobsters sponsoring him. Their match in Chicago on September 25, 1962, lasted for just two minutes and six seconds—ended by one of the fastest knockouts in boxing history. The ex-con knocked out the heavyweight champ in the first round to become the new titleholder. Fans across the country were appalled that a boxer with a criminal past could be hailed as a champion.

Patterson wanted a rematch; outspoken fans did too. Madison Square Garden rejected the fight because of Liston's alleged Mob ties, throwing a national spotlight on the fight's future. In 1963, Mob ties were no obstacle in Las Vegas. Liston the champ faced off against Patterson on July 22, 1963 at the Las Vegas Convention Center. Emotions ran high; fortunes were staked at every betting window in town.

This time, Patterson lasted a mere four seconds longer, knocked out again in Round One. Liston retained the title. On the *Tonight Show*, Johnny Carson joked that Patterson's promoters should sell advertising on the soles of his shoes.

Muhammad Ali vs. Floyd Patterson, Las Vegas Convention Center
November 22, 1965

A gold medal winner at the 1960 Olympics, the cocky young Cassius Clay defeated Sonny Liston in 1964 to become the new heavyweight champion. Next up: Las Vegas, where Clay would face the ex-champ Floyd Patterson.

First, Clay made the controversial decision to convert to the Islamic faith. He changed his name to Muhammad Ali, a shocker in Judeo-Christian America. Patterson fueled the controversy. "The image of a Black Muslim as the world heavyweight champion disgraces the sport and the nation," he stated bluntly in *Sports Illustrated* in October 1965. Even Frank Sinatra weighed in, affirming that Patterson was the one "fighting for America."

The gate took in over $3.5 million (about $24 million in 2010 dollars). More money flowed from high-priced closed-circuit television contracts. Multi-million-dollar purses were guaranteed to both opponents.

In the ring, Ali got even. Early on, it became apparent that he could knock out Patterson with one solid punch, but he did not. Instead, Ali mocked Patterson, calling him "Uncle Tom" and yelling "Get me a contender," landing just enough punches to keep Patterson on his feet for 12 rounds. Though Ali retained the title, the crowd booed.

Muhammad Ali returned to Las Vegas five more times to defend his heavyweight title. His heavily promoted events at Caesars Palace, the Convention Center and the Hilton established Las Vegas as the boxing capital of the world.

Mike Tyson vs. Evander Holyfield, MGM Grand
November 9, 1996

In a 1986 title fight at the Las Vegas Hilton, 20-year-old Mike Tyson became the youngest boxer in history to win the heavyweight championship. His ferocious boxing style earned him the nickname the "Baddest Man on the Planet."

In 1992, a rape conviction sent him to prison in Indiana for three years. Before and during Tyson's incarceration, Evander Holyfield was the reigning heavyweight champ. Following his release from prison, Tyson made an impressive comeback, winning the heavyweight championship from Frank Bruno at the MGM Grand in March 1996. In November, Tyson, the 28-year-old two-time champ, would return to the MGM Grand to face ex-champ Evander Holyfield.

Sports pundits viewed 34-year-old Holyfield, also a two-time champ, as the underdog, with little chance of winning. Holyfield surprised them all, defeating Tyson in a technical knockout in the 11th round. He made history, tying with Muhammad Ali as the only boxers to win the heavyweight championship belt three times. (He'd break the record by winning a fourth time, in December 2000, at the Paris Las Vegas.)

The pundits turned this bout into a referendum on Tyson instead, opining that his personal life had taken its toll; he wasn't the same ferocious player. The Baddest Man on the Planet demanded a rematch immediately.

Mike Tyson vs. Evander Holyfield, MGM Grand
June 28, 1997

The rematch at the MGM Grand less than one year later was an even bigger event than the first face-off, promoted as "The Sound and the Fury." Tyson was paid $30 million and Holyfield received $35 million, the biggest purses in boxing history at the time. It was also one of the most shocking events in modern sports.

By the third round, it became apparent to Tyson that he wasn't winning. In a ferocious act Tyson clamed was in response to a headbutt, he attacked and bit off a piece of his opponent's ear. There was blood in the ring as he spat out a piece of Holyfield's flesh. After a doctor declared Holyfield fit to fight, the brawl resumed, and when the two fighters clinched arms again, Tyson bit Holyfield's other ear. As the bell rang to end the round, Tyson attacked Holyfield's corner.

The fight was stopped, and Tyson was disqualified. Holyfield was proclaimed the winner, and the arena erupted into a near riot.

"He planned this," Tyson's former trainer Teddy Atlas told the *NY Daily News*. He predicted that Tyson would be disqualified in an attempt to go out on his own terms. "In his world, he would be known as savage and brutal."

The Nevada State Boxing Commission immediately withheld $3 million from Tyson's purse, the legal maximum at the time. The vote was unanimous to rescind Tyson's boxing license. He was fined $3 million and ordered to pay all legal costs.

With cries of "Cannibalism," Tyson was condemned in the media, and the Sweet Science underwent harsh scrutiny. One year later, Tyson's license was restored and he returned to the ring.

1 Convention Center: 3150 Paradise Road
2 Caesars Palace: 3570 Las Vegas Blvd. S.
3 Hilton: 3000 Paradise Rd.
4 MGM Grand: 3799 Las Vegas Blvd. S.
5 Mandalay Bay: 3950 Las Vegas Blvd. S.
6 Thomas & Mack Center at the University of Nevada at Las Vegas: 4505 S. Maryland Parkway

■ Existing Building
■ Building no longer exists

CHAPTER 22.

HOWARD HUGHES

In 1967, Howard Hughes was so famous that when he applied for a Nevada Gaming License, his fingerprints weren't necessary. Good thing too, because the recluse also refused to be photographed and wouldn't submit to the financial background check that was required by state law. The state gave him the license anyway. What came next changed Las Vegas forever.

From his mother, Hughes inherited an obsessive-compulsive fear of germs. Ailene Hughes was extremely germ-phobic. She examined her son every day for diseases and was cautious about what he ate, terrified that he might catch polio. The fear of germs eventually consumed Howard as well, the source of dementia in his final years.

Upon receiving his inheritance, Hughes dropped out of Rice College, took it directly to Hollywood, invested in RKO Studios and produced several hit films. He made a star of Jean Harlow and invented a special brassiere for Jane Russell. He dated many famous women, including Ava Gardner, Lana Turner, Katharine Hepburn, Ginger Rogers; he allegedly proposed to Joan Fontaine, and he married Jean Peters. Dashingly

Howard Hughes on the set of *Hell's Angels*, circa 1928-1930

handsome and incredibly rich, Hughes was a frequent subject for
gossip columnists.

But it was Hughes's other obsession—aviation—that would make him
a celebrity. Hughes was a daring pilot who set the world speed record in
1935 in an aircraft of his own design. When he flew around the world
in 1937, in the record-setting time of 91 hours, *Time* magazine reported
that his ticker tape parade in lower Manhattan "surpassed Lindbergh's."
President Franklin D. Roosevelt presented him with a trophy. In 1939,
Hughes was awarded with a Congressional Gold Medal for "advancing
the science of aviation and thus bringing great credit to his country
throughout the world."

By 1966, Howard Hughes's fortune was nearly $2 billion, with income generated from Hughes Aircraft, the oil industry, mining investments (he was the largest landowner in Clark County, with 27,000 acres of mines) and electronics he manufactured for the Air Force. When he sold his 78 percent stake in Trans World Airlines for $566 million, Howard Hughes was flush with cash to invest. Next stop: Las Vegas.

Residents of Nevada paid no personal or corporate income tax, no inheritance tax, no franchise tax, no warehouse tax, and real estate taxes were limited by the state constitution. The sales tax was only 3 percent. Casino taxes paid for 30 percent of the state's expenses. For an enterprising man with millions to invest (the interest alone on Hughes's TWA proceeds was $85,000 a day), Nevada looked mighty appealing.

On Thanksgiving Day, at four in the morning, a train deposited 60-year-old Howard Hughes and his entourage at a desolate crossing in North Las Vegas. He was six-foot-two, an anemic 150 pounds, and addicted to codeine to relieve the back pain caused by aircraft accidents years earlier. From the train tracks, he was whisked away to Moe Dalitz's place, the Desert Inn. Accommodations were arranged by an old acquaintance, newspaper publisher Hank Greenspun; Hughes and company would occupy the entire eighth and ninth floors.

His companions were a team of Mormon caretakers Hughes retained to oversee his finances, his legal matters, and fulfill his orders regarding comfort and privacy. Nicknamed the Mormon Mafia, they were practically the only people to see Hughes during the four years that he made Las Vegas his home. The observant Mormons didn't drink, smoke or gamble, which made them trustworthy employees for Mr. Hughes, but deadbeats to Dalitz.

Dalitz was initially thrilled to have one of the world's few billionaires living under the roof of his Desert Inn, but he stopped smiling when he realized that Hughes was too phobic to leave the rooms, had no plans for departure, and that his team had no intention of gambling. With the holidays approaching, high rollers were coming to town. Dalitz needed his suites back. But how do you evict Howard Hughes? Dalitz contacted Hank Greenspun.

Negotiations ensued. Hughes wasn't going to pack up overnight; he had no place to go. Greenspun served as the intermediary, reporting to Dalitz. Exasperated after just a few days, Greenspun asked Hughes, "Why don't you just *buy* the hotel?"

That was the solution. Hughes's bid for the Desert Inn could not have come at a better time. Detrimental stories about organized crime in Las Vegas abounded. To state officials, Howard Hughes was a shining knight: a well-respected entrepreneur with one of the largest bankrolls on earth, and with an image that could instantly redeem the city from its stigma. On April 1, 1967, title to the Desert Inn officially passed from Moe Dalitz and his partners to Howard Hughes. As the Gaming Board Chairman put it: "Frankly, we waived things for him."

Hughes went to work with renewed vigor. In a memo to his aides, he crowed: "I want to acquire even more hotels and make Las Vegas as trustworthy and respectable as the New York Stock Exchange." Next, Hughes went shopping on Las Vegas Boulevard.

The city's original investors were now in their 60s and 70s, and they were eager to cash out. Hughes spent $70 million that summer; even the town that had seen its share of high rollers was left a little breathless. He bought the Sands, the Frontier and the Castaways. He paid to finish construction of the Landmark. The Silver Slipper was a small casino across from the Desert Inn. Hughes complained that its revolving neon slipper disturbed his sleep, so he bought that hotel too.

Nevada's Governor Paul Laxalt was Hughes's biggest fan: "His coming here did things for our state image that a multimillion-dollar public relations campaign couldn't have achieved. He has given Nevada gaming instant respectability."

George Franklin, Jr., the Clark County District Attorney added: "By buying out certain hotels, [Hughes] retired some of our more dubious characters, and we are very grateful."

Officials were grateful; columnists praised him, but tourists wondered if Hughes even existed. Nobody saw the man. He spent days in total seclusion, apparently careening between lucidity and dementia. His eccentricities were endless. Hughes only had his hair cut and nails trimmed once a year. Aides weren't permitted to make eye contact with him. To avoid germs, Hughes insisted that everyone use tissues to pick up or hand objects to him. He didn't trust a soul.

But Hughes wasn't the only problem. No one in his organization knew how to run a gambling operation. As Hughes acquired resorts, Robert Maheu, his most trusted confidante, kept most of the Mob-connected managers on the payroll. The Skim continued as always, only now Hughes was being defrauded along with the IRS.

In February 1970, Hughes received a tip from federal investigators looking into Las Vegas corruption. Maheu was allegedly involved in kickback schemes, also turning a blind eye to the Skim. At the Sands, state officials turned up $186,000 in markers, some signed with fictitious names. Maheu wanted to write off the $186,000 as a bad debt, which the state officials bluntly refused.

Many of Hughes's enterprises were not paying off in the manner his accountants originally projected; some were barely breaking even. It was apparent that some of the casinos' funds were going into the pockets of employees within the Hughes organization. Most suspiciously, the operating expenses of the Maheu-managed properties were far higher than his other enterprises.

Hughes ordered a small army of attorneys, auditors and casino experts to examine his gambling operations. To avoid the legal showdown with his most-trusted employee, it was time for Hughes to leave Las Vegas. On Thanksgiving 1970, exactly four years to the day after his arrival, Howard Hughes and his aides relocated to Paradise Island in the Bahamas. Though Governor Laxalt tried to assure everyone that he was just vacationing, Hughes never returned.

Maheu was fired in December 1970. He filed a libel suit soon after, collecting $2.8 million dollars. He died in Las Vegas in 2008 at age 90.

Howard Hughes died on a plane trip from Acapulco to the Methodist Hospital in Houston on April 5, 1976. An autopsy determined that he died of kidney failure caused by malnutrition and drug use. His tall frame weighed barely 90 pounds. X-rays revealed five broken hypodermic needles in his arms. To inject codeine into his muscles, Hughes had used glass syringes with metal needles that easily became detached. He was buried in Houston, Texas, beside his parents.

As the state officials predicted, Howard Hughes's investments legitimized Las Vegas, ushering in a new era of possibilities. It took someone who was a little crazy to willingly mire himself in the machinations of the Mob, and it didn't hurt that he was a billionaire too. Hughes's buyouts provided a convenient retirement for the town's most conspicuous wise guys, fulfilling at least part of his vow to make Las Vegas "trustworthy and respectable." Most importantly, thanks to Hughes, the gaming laws were changed to permit corporations, not just individuals, to obtain licenses. At last, companies like Hyatt, Hilton, Ramada and Holiday Inn, respected hoteliers that had avoided Las Vegas when crime syndicates ran the town, saw potential in Nevada. With even greater amounts of capital to invest, these corporations demolished each of Hughes's hotels to invent a completely new, corporate, Las Vegas.

1. Desert Inn: 3145 Las Vegas Blvd. S.
2. The Sands: 3355 Las Vegas Blvd. S.
3. The Frontier: 3120 Las Vegas Blvd. S.
4. The Castaways: 3210 S. 5th Street
5. Landmark: corner of Paradise Rd. and Convention Center Dr.
6. Silver Slipper: 3100 Las Vegas Blvd. S.
7. North Las Vegas Airport

Existing Building
Building No Longer Exists

CHAPTER 23.

LIBERACE

In 1955, Liberace, the celebrated pianist and showman, set a world record. At the brand new Riviera, the Strip's first high-rise building, Liberace was paid the astronomical salary of $55,000 a week, making him the highest-paid performer *on earth*.

On a giant stage, Liberace's show was all spectacle: Chinese acrobats soared and dancing girls kicked. The performance peaked with Liberace himself, playing on a piano encrusted with thousands of tiny mirrors. The act literally dazzled. His show continued at the Riviera for years, where he'd return each season with a completely new production, striving to outdo his already over-the-top reputation. He'd strut onstage in feathers, in hot pants, in a $60,000 chinchilla coat with a train, in a tuxedo jacket that shimmered with nearly a million and a half hand-sewn sequins; he even commissioned one rhinestone-studded cape that weighed over 100 pounds. The rest of the show was pretty terrific too. For the 1963 season, Liberace's warm-up act at the Riviera was an up-and-coming singer named Barbra Streisand.

← Liberace in the early 1970s

In an era when Las Vegas resorts were still being carved out of the scorched desert earth, and most shows featured a single comic, magician or singer in an intimate setting, the jaw-dropping scale of Liberace's productions turned his show into the Strip's best-known landmark. He had an infectious rapport with his audiences, taking requests and cracking jokes spontaneously. "I'm happiest when I'm onstage," he later confided, "because that's when I'm in complete control."

Offstage, his life was a collection of showbiz clichés. Wladziu (Walter) Liberace's mother was a Polish immigrant who encouraged the sensitive boy to explore all facets of music. As a teenager, he earned a job as the piano player for silent movies in Milwaukee, Wisconsin. His hot-tempered father, an Italian immigrant and classically trained French horn player, disapproved because the boy wasn't playing the classics. Liberace kept his job, because his salary of 50 cents a week was desperately needed to support the penniless family of six. The tension between father and son increased when Walter attended a concert and unexpectedly spotted his father in the audience, two rows ahead with his mistress. It was one of Liberace's earliest secrets.

Both parents agreed on one thing: the boy had a prodigious talent for the piano. He secured a scholarship at the Wisconsin College of Music while still attending high school. During the Great Depression, 16-year-old Liberace brought home a significant paycheck when he debuted with the Chicago Symphony as the soloist for Liszt's "Concerto in A Major." Years later, in his memoir *The Wonderful Private World of Liberace*, he noted the mood of the country during those hard times: "The luxury of serious music was one of the first things eliminated by the public. They didn't feel it was a necessary commodity, and attendance fell off." The enterprising Walter Liberace became the piano whiz "Walter Busterkeys" who went to work in nightclubs and bars in Milwaukee. "There's more money in being commercial," he stated more than once. It's the mantra that defined his career.

Liberace toured American cities briefly as a classical pianist but struggled to make it in New York. That's when he made the conscious decision to put on a show, not a concert. He devised a specialty act that he laughingly called "classical music with the boring parts left out." He'd play Chopin but mix in elements from "Home on the Range;" he'd dive into the "Minute Waltz," racing against a clock to complete the piece in 37 seconds.

Life changed for Liberace in 1944, when he booked his act at the Last Frontier on the Las Vegas Strip. The engagement went so well that when he was offered a long-term contract, he dropped Walter from his name, told his friends and family to call him Lee, and continued to perform at the Last Frontier for nearly a decade.

Meanwhile, television beckoned. In 1953, Liberace's syndicated television series was sold to scores of local markets across the United States. With his mother seated in the studio audience, he played the piano directly to the camera, illuminated by a candelabrum that immediately became his trademark. In the 1950s, when most televisions received fewer than 10 channels, his single name became a household word. Television made Liberace both popular and prosperous. His first two years' earnings from television netted him $7 million. Royalties continued for years as the shows ran in syndication.

Music critics were harsh. The *New York Times* bemoaned Liberace's lack of respect for composers. "Liberace recreates—if that is the word—each composition in his own image. When it is too difficult, he simplifies it. When it is too simple, he complicates it."

Liberace responded with characteristic humor: "I cried...all the way to the bank!" Years later, he told Johnny Carson on the *Tonight Show*, "You know that bank I used to cry all the way to?" Pause. "I bought it."

Liberace in the film *When the Boys Meet the Girls*, 1965

The clichés continued. The boy who grew up in poverty struck it rich. He bought homes in Las Vegas and Beverly Hills. He installed a swimming pool in the shape of a grand piano. Overcompensating for years of going without, he now spent staggering amounts on material possessions. He amassed over a dozen grand pianos in his Las Vegas residence, each one gaudier than the next. He spent a fortune on his flamboyant wardrobe, bought jeweled rings for every finger, acquired several Rolls Royces and gained respect as an exceptionally generous philanthropist.

Loyal fans visiting Las Vegas perceived Liberace's sparkling acquisitions as the height of glamour. They dubbed him "Mr. Showmanship." Liberace reigned on the Las Vegas Strip for nearly four decades, performing in many of the city's greatest venues, from the Moulin Rouge in its heyday, to the Sahara, Caesars Palace and the MGM Grand. In 1971, he was offered the astonishing salary of $300,000 a week to alternate between the Las Vegas Hilton and the Lake Tahoe Hilton, where he bought yet another home.

Along the way, his secrets were protected. In London in 1959, he won a libel suit against a *Daily Mirror* columnist who described him as "fruit-flavored." Asked on the witness stand for his stance on homosexuality, Liberace testified that it "offends convention and offends society."

He lied. The truth about Liberace's secret orientation would have ended his career. In the repressive 1950s and '60s, lives were shattered when people were exposed as gay. At first, Liberace battled his secret as a devout Catholic. Even in the permissive 1970s, he stayed mum about his personal life. The threat of perjury from that lawsuit kept Liberace in the closet. "I can't admit a thing," he confided to his lover Scott Thorson, "unless I want to be known as the world's biggest liar."

The 58-year-old Liberace had met Thorson in 1977. Thorson was a barely-legal young man who survived a life in orphanages and foster homes for most of his 18 years. Liberace paid for Thorson, a veterinarian's assistant in Los Angeles, to fly to Las Vegas to deliver medication for his poodle. Months later, Thorson moved out of his foster parents' home and into the life of Liberace. As Thorson wrote in his book *Behind the Candelabra: My Life With Liberace*, "Lee, the man, didn't attract me. However, the glitz and glitter of Vegas did."

There was always another title to explain Liberace's boy toy on the payroll, as a chauffeur, valet and even bodyguard. Liberace was so smitten that he planned to adopt his gay lover as his son. First, however, 20-year-old Thorson would need to undergo plastic surgery…to resemble Liberace in his youth.

The surgery went well, but the repercussions didn't. Thorson developed a taste for recreational drugs that he claims were prescribed by Liberace's secretive plastic surgeon. Cocaine, Quaaludes and Demerol gave Thorson a psychological escape while living as Liberace's companion for five years. In 1982, when Liberace threw him out, a publicity-seeking (and later disbarred) attorney told Thorson about "palimony" and then sued Liberace for $112 million on Thorson's behalf. They wrangled in and out of court for years, then reached a settlement for far less in 1984. After decades of concealing his private life, Liberace was outed at age 63.

Gay or not, Liberace's devoted fans still loved him. He continued to fill giant-sized theaters. In New York, he grossed $2.5 million, playing 18 concerts in 21 days at Radio City Music Hall, with a final performance on November 2, 1986. As *Time* reported it: "Liberace announced that he was going on vacation for a while. What he was really doing was going out on top."

Liberace had known since 1985 that he was HIV-positive. Twelve weeks after the Radio City success, on February 4, 1987, Liberace died at his home in Palm Springs, California. In a futile attempt to protect Liberace's legacy, his doctor entered "cardiac failure" on the death certificate. Hours after Liberace's body was embalmed, the coroner formally rejected the death certificate. An autopsy was ordered, as required when there is suspicion of a contagious disease. The autopsy report confirmed that Liberace died of complications of AIDS.

In 1976, he had created the Liberace Foundation for the Performing and Creative Arts, awarding scholarships to students at American universities and conservatories. Upon his death, 90 percent of his estate was bequeathed to his foundation. In its first 30 years, nearly 3,000 students have benefited from his generosity.

Liberace introduced spectacle to the Las Vegas Strip with a style that cannot be duplicated. Big-name entertainers are reluctant to devote decades to the crowds in Las Vegas, and nowhere in the entertainment industry is there a headliner whose career spanned 40 years without a single dip. Liberace proved that in American pop culture, there can be only one Mr. Showmanship.

1 Last Frontier: 3120 Las Vegas Blvd. S.
2 Riviera: 2901 Las Vegas Blvd. S.
3 Moulin Rouge: 900 W. Bonanza Road
4 Liberace Museum / Foundation for the Performing and Creative Arts: 1775 East Tropicana Ave.
5 The Sahara: 2535 Las Vegas Blvd. S.
6 Caesars Palace: 3570 Las Vegas Blvd. S.
7 MGM Grand: 3645 Las Vegas Blvd. S.
8 Las Vegas Hilton: 3000 Paradise Rd.

Existing Building
Building No Longer Exists

CHAPTER 24.

ELVIS

In 1970, Elvis Presley was the only star big enough to break his own attendance records. Decked out in sequins and rhinestones, the King of Rock and Roll reached the pinnacle of his career in Las Vegas…and the town is still talking about it. Decades later, iconic images (and more than a few impersonators) abound.

Presley's Las Vegas debut in 1956 was a much different story. He turned 21 that January; then RCA Victor released his first album in March. *Elvis Presley* made history as the first rock and roll album ever to top the *Billboard* chart. Even more impressively, *Elvis Presley* kept rock and roll at the top of that chart for 10 solid weeks. Suddenly, Presley wasn't just a singer; he was national news.

Sammy Lewis, the entertainment buyer for the New Frontier in Las Vegas, was attracted to performers in the news. He struck a deal with Colonel Tom Parker, Presley's promoter (who was never really a Colonel): When Frank Sinatra's engagement ended in April, they'd present Elvis Presley live at the New Frontier. He'd play a 12-minute set

← Elvis Presley in *Viva Las Vegas*, 1964

twice each night for 14 nights, sharing the bill with comedian Shecky Greene, plus Freddy Martin and his orchestra.

In 1956, Las Vegas was euphoric over the atomic bombs exploding at the Nevada Proving Ground nearby. Lewis and the Colonel decided to introduce Elvis Presley as "The Atomic Powered Singer." They erected a 24-foot-tall cutout of Presley outside the New Frontier Hotel, and then the Colonel fitted him with a bow tie and jacket. On April 23, 1956, with his record still at the top of the chart, Elvis Presley stepped onstage at the New Frontier.

"He was kind of weird-looking for those people," recalled Freddie Bell, who performed in the New Frontier's lounge. "He had the sideburns and that hair. And he was singing rock and roll, loudly, in Frank's town. Elvis was too loud for Vegas then."

Liberace and Vampira were in the opening night audience. "There was much hip-thrusting, you know," Vampira recalled to Mike Weatherford in his book *Cult Vegas*. "The audience was stunned because they didn't know what to make of it. Finally, somebody booed. And then everyone started to boo."

As *Newsweek* described it, Presley's act went down "like a jug of corn liquor at a champagne party." Shecky Greene concurred: "The presentation was terrible. It looked like a rehearsal. He wasn't ready."

But Presley didn't need Las Vegas in 1956. He'd already signed the contract with Paramount to star in his first picture, *Love Me Tender*. Then, on September 9, about 60 million viewers tuned in to watch him on *The Ed Sullivan Show*, an astounding 82.6 percent of the television audience. A new star with a new sound challenged Sinatra for the top spot on the *Billboard* charts. For two brief weeks at the New Frontier, Presley showed mainstream America that rock and roll had arrived.

Despite the harsh reception, Presley discovered that he actually enjoyed Las Vegas. He'd return often over the next decade to relax, to film, and to marry a young Priscilla Ann Wagner at the Aladdin Hotel. But he wouldn't venture onto a Las Vegas stage again for 13 years.

By 1968, Elvis Presley had served in the army, appeared in 31 films, and released nine studio albums, 18 soundtracks and 156 singles. Although Colonel Parker had little knowledge of filmmaking, he pushed Presley through a heavy schedule of modestly budgeted musical comedies, with some feeble songs that Presley didn't even want to sing. When Presley's soundtrack album *Speedway* died at number 82 on the pop charts, he told the Colonel it was time to get back in touch with his audience. He wanted to return to television.

The special that aired on December 3, 1968 was called simply *Elvis*, but soon became known as the Comeback Special, taped at Presley's first live performances since 1961.

Mounting the show wasn't easy; Colonel Parker despised producer/ director Steve Binder, who challenged his every decision. Fortunately, Binder won. Presley did not appear in a tuxedo to croon "Silent Night" as Parker had planned. Instead, the uninhibited live segments showcased Presley in tight black leather, singing and playing guitar, yanking his audiences past Parker's forgettable movies and back to Presley's vibrant rock and roll days. The show was NBC's highest-rated program that season; the soundtrack album landed in the top 10 on the *Billboard* charts. "There is something magical about watching a man who has lost himself find his way back home," wrote reviewer Jon Landau in *Eye* magazine. "He sang with the kind of power people no longer expect of rock 'n' roll singers."

To which the Colonel added: "You know, we can take that show you just did, put it in Vegas, and make a lot of money."

Elvis Presley, 1972

Presley reportedly shrugged and said, "Sounds like we're playing Vegas."

In 1969, billionaire Kirk Kerkorian opened the International Hotel in Las Vegas. The largest hotel in the world, it also featured the largest showroom in Las Vegas, with nearly 2,000 seats. Fresh from winning her first Oscar, Barbra Streisand opened the club, winning stellar reviews, as did the clubroom and the new hotel. Two weeks later, Presley returned to the concert stage, performing at the International for 58 consecutive sold-out shows, breaking all Las Vegas attendance records. The critics and the public raved; Presley was back on his game.

Presley had done his homework; he knew that a Las Vegas appearance was a chance to reinvent himself. In 1969, Tom Jones was the most popular singer in Las Vegas. Unbuttoned to the navel, the gyrating Welshman generated such sexual energy that screaming women threw underwear and hotel room keys onstage during his shows. He and Presley had been friends since they filmed *Paradise, Hawaiian Style* at Paramount. Now, as Presley studied his friend's live performance, his new stage persona took shape. Presley put karate kicks, brassy arrangements and blatant sex appeal into his act.

He hired Sammy Shore as his warm-up act, the same comedian who had opened for Tom Jones. Then the curtain rose on Presley, clad in black, clutching his acoustic guitar, and backed by a rock band, a stage orchestra, plus male and female gospel choirs. The 15-song show ended with a brass-powered version of "Suspicious Minds," Presley's most recent single (his first in seven years to reach number one on the charts, and his last).

He reveled in this chance to connect with live audiences again. As he confessed at the news conference that followed his landmark opening night: "It was getting harder and harder to perform to a movie camera."

The very next day, the hotel president struck a deal with Colonel Parker: Presley would play two engagements per year, at $125,000 per week. Kerkorian built the Imperial Suite, a special penthouse on the 30th floor for Presley's Las Vegas residence. Presley's productions would return twice annually for the next seven years.

At the next engagement in February 1970, attired in a sequined jumpsuit, Presley broke his own attendance record. He shattered that record again in August 1970, and then topped it in August 1972.

By performing two shows nightly, he delivered 4,000 potential gamblers to the International's casino every night. One year after the grand opening, Kerkorian cashed out, selling his hugely successful enterprise to the Hilton Hotel chain. (It's today's Las Vegas Hilton). Presley couldn't get any bigger; the Hilton had the only facility large enough to accommodate the crowds.

Now divorced, Presley partied hard when he was offstage, and rocked hard when he was onstage. Though his costumes became more outlandish, now including an American Eagle cape, they could no longer conceal Presley's bloated appearance.

Lamar Fike from Presley's entourage saw how hard Presley worked for the money. "Do you realize what kind of hell four weeks is? That's a marathon – nearly 60 performances. And Elvis had such a high-energy show that when he would do an honest hour and 15 minutes twice a night, he was so tired he was cross-eyed. That's why he took all that stuff to keep him going."

Las Vegas doctors helped Presley maintain his pace. As the shows got sloppy, rumors surfaced that Presley was strung out. He responded directly onstage: "I have never been strung out on anything in my life, except music."

But that wasn't true. He denied his abuse of amphetamines and narcotics because his doctors had prescribed them. Then shows were canceled. Citing "fatigue," Presley was hospitalized five times between 1973 and 1975. His multiple ailments—glaucoma, high blood pressure, liver damage and an enlarged colon—were all aggravated by drug abuse.

On August 16, 1977, Presley was scheduled to fly out of Memphis to begin another tour. Instead, his girlfriend found him unconscious on the bathroom floor. Death was officially pronounced at 3:30 p.m. Elvis Presley was 42 years old.

That night in Las Vegas, rain fell in torrents, an inch and a half in just three hours. The entire city, it seemed, mourned the loss of its king.

1. New Frontier: 3120 Las Vegas Blvd. S.
2. Aladdin Hotel: 3667 Las Vegas Blvd. S.
3. International Hotel: 3000 Paradise Rd.
4. The Flamingo: 3555 Las Vegas Blvd. S.

Existing Building
Building No Longer Exists

CHAPTER 25.

SIEGFRIED AND ROY

On a German ocean liner in 1959, 20-year-old Siegfried Fischbacher, the cabin steward, met 15-year-old Roy Horn, the waiter. Forty years later, Siegfried and Roy were hailed as "Masters of the Impossible" in Las Vegas, the ninth highest-paid celebrities in the United States, directly behind movie director Steven Spielberg.

Siegfried Fischbacher came from Bavaria and wanted to be a magician. He performed magic acts on the ocean liner in 1959, then asked the young waiter from Oldenburg for his opinion. "Predictable," Roy reportedly responded. "If you can make doves disappear, why not a *cheetah*?" Conveniently, Roy was an experienced handler of Chico, the cheetah at the Bremen Zoo. With Roy's skill at handling exotic animals, the pair had an act unlike any other.

← Siegfried and Roy, 1994, with one of their rare Royal White Tigers

The friends became lovers, and the lovers became business partners. They never denied their intimate relationship, but by the time they reached Las Vegas, the business relationship came first. Siegfried and Roy were showmen devoted to a death-defying craft.

First, they worked their way through Europe, billed as Siegfried and Partner, adding large beasts to the act. Following successful engagements at the Folies Bergère in Paris, they made the leap to Las Vegas.

Siegfried & Roy first appeared at the Tropicana in 1967, presenting a specialty act with smoothly choreographed illusions. They put exotic animals through their paces, then made them disappear. Show bookers across the Strip were skeptical; they held little faith that magic could be profitable in Las Vegas showrooms.

"When we first started here, magic was always shoved to the back of the show. It never went on the marquee," Siegfried later told a reporter. "Now almost every major showroom has a magic act. Magic is in."

Those skeptical bookers soon clamored to hire the act that would redefine entertainment in Las Vegas: Siegfried and Roy ushered in the era of family-friendly shows. No Rat Pack here, but a dazzling cat pack, including Roy's signature white tigers, in stunning illusions suitable for all ages. Siegfried and Roy performed over 5,700 times in Las Vegas, premiering their new acts at the old MGM Grand, the Stardust and the Frontier. Their success paved the way for elaborate magic acts that followed everywhere on the Strip, where stars like Criss Angel, Penn and Teller, David Copperfield, Doug Henning, Harry Blackstone and Lance Burton welcomed a steady clientele. The act at the top of the pay scale was consistently Siegfried and Roy.

In 1972, the illusionists received an award for the Best Show of the Year. In 1990, they accepted Steve Wynn's lifetime contract to appear (or as their slogan said: "disappear") at the Mirage for $57.5 million a year.

Wynn built the Jungle Palace at the Mirage, a park and habitat for the act's 60-odd big cats, plus residential quarters for Siegfried and Roy. (Siegfried owned another residence in a gated community too.)

How do you tame a tiger? Until the cats were a year old, they slept in bed with Roy, who bottle-fed each animal to gain its trust. As performers, the cats all had a personal relationship with Roy, their constant co-star and friend. By day, they languished in the Secret Garden at the Mirage, where visitors paid to see endangered animals in a simulation of their natural environment.

A short distance from Las Vegas, Siegfried and Roy built a 100-acre estate they named Little Bavaria. Filled with antiques they collected from around the world, the compound included housing for guests, housing for animals and a pool where Roy swam with the cats. Roy blissfully reflected to a reporter: "Siegfried and I are living a modern poem."

Still, they had their detractors, including People for the Ethical Treatment of Animals. "A Las Vegas stage is not a natural home for an exotic animal," PETA vice-president Dan Mathews cautioned.

But Siegfried and Roy were also active conservationists who protected and preserved endangered animals. The white tigers, native to India, were nearly extinct until the illusionists founded the "Living Classroom," a breeding program at the Zoological Society of Cincinnati. They nurtured a family of rare animals that grew into 40 big cats. Siegfried and Roy named them the "Royal White Tigers of Nevada."

In 1994, Siegfried and Roy were asked by the South African government to set up a similar breeding program for lions, specifically the endangered White Lions of Timbavati. Not only were there no more white lions in the wild, according to specialists in Johannesburg, but only an alarming 10 remained in captivity. Siegfried and Roy helped to increase that number to 18. Soon, 11 white lions lived in Las Vegas.

A white tiger at Siegfried and Roy's Secret Garden at the Mirage

But even with the pair's experience, danger comes with wild animals. "There's a mantra that Roy always repeated: 'Never turn your back on these animals.' Every night, he realized he took his life in his hands," television reporter Robin Leach recalled.

In his 1992 book *Mastering the Impossible,* Roy describes a frightening incident. "After playing and rolling in the grass, [a tiger] suddenly... pinned me down. Our eyes met and instantly I knew she wasn't playing anymore – in a split second, she would bite. I raised my head and bit her as hard as I could on her nose. And she never attempted to bite me again."

On October 3, 2003, Roy's 59th birthday, the act did not go as planned. It was a tightly paced 95-minute show with costumed dancers, laser lights, lions, tigers and masterful illusions. During one of the quietest moments in the show, Roy came onstage with Montecore, a 7-year-old white tiger, to explain his work in preserving these rare animals. Montecore was trained to lie down, then stand with his paws on Roy's shoulders in a sort of embrace. They had been doing this act together for over five years.

According to Mirage owner Steve Wynn, there was a woman with a "big hairdo" in the front row who "distracted" Montecore. When she reached out, apparently to pet the animal, Roy jumped between the woman and the tiger to regain the cat's eye contact. The cat growled. Roy chided it and pulled on the tiger's chain. Returning to the routine, he told the tiger to lie down…but Montecore didn't. He grabbed Roy's arm instead. According to Wynn, Roy bopped Montecore on the nose with the microphone, saying, "Release. Release." Then Roy tripped over the cat's paw and fell on his back. Witnesses say the cat pounced, biting into Roy's neck. Stagehands rushed onstage and jumped on the cat. "It was only then," Wynn said, "that the confused tiger leaned over Roy and attempted to carry him off the stage to safety."

As Siegfried would later explain on the *Larry King* show, Montecore had no way of knowing that Roy, unlike a tiger cub, did not have fur and thick skin covering his neck, leaving him vulnerable to injury. If Montecore wanted to injure Roy, he would have snapped Roy's neck and shaken him back and forth.

Aides backstage were extremely prepared, even though they had never faced this crisis before. Stagehands sprayed Roy and Montecore with a fire extinguisher to separate them. Releasing Roy, Montecore retired to his cage. Roy was rushed to the University Medical Center. He was critically injured, yet he instinctively instructed everyone, "Don't shoot the cat!"

Meanwhile, the audience sat stunned, wondering if they were witnessing another illusion, this time with blood. Then Siegfried stepped onstage, hastily announcing that the rest of the show was canceled. His 13-year run at the Mirage, and his 44-year career with Roy, ended on that tragic night.

Roy was in critical condition for weeks, suffering a stroke and partial paralysis. Doctors removed one quarter of his skull to relieve the pressure on his swelling brain. Eventually, he was transferred to UCLA Medical Center in Los Angeles for long-term recovery and rehabilitation. With extensive therapy, Roy was able to overcome some of his injuries.

In February 2009, Siegfried and Roy returned for one "final" appearance with now 12-year-old Montecore as a benefit for the Lou Ruvo Brain Institute being built in Las Vegas. The 10-minute program was recorded, then broadcast on the television program *20/20*. It featured one of Siegfried and Roy's signature illusions, in which Siegfried and Montecore magically switched places from within separate, locked transparent enclosures.

On April 23, 2010, Siegfried and Roy officially retired from show business. Their longtime manager Bernie Yuman stated for the record: "The last time we closed, we didn't have a lot of warning. This is farewell. This is the dot at the end of the sentence."

1. Tropicana: 3801 Las Vegas Blvd. S.
2. MGM Grand: 3645 Las Vegas Blvd. S.
3. Stardust: 3000 Las Vegas Blvd. S.
4. Frontier: 3120 Las Vegas Blvd. S.
5. The Mirage: 3400 Las Vegas Blvd. S.
6. Cleveland Clinic Lou Ruvo Center for Brain Health:
   888 West Bonneville Ave.

■ Existing Building
■ Building No Longer Exists

CHAPTER 26.

MIT CONQUERS LAS VEGAS

In 1958, mathematics professor Edward Thorp beat the system. At the Massachusetts Institute of Technology, he calculated a mathematical proof: by counting cards, players can gain an advantage over the house in blackjack games. This development set the stage for a swindle that thrived for four decades — until it all came crashing down.

After analyzing data from millions of blackjack simulations played on early computers, Professor Thorp published his results in 1962. His popular book *Beat the Dealer* explained the strategy for playing blackjack: the house's odds diminish as the dealers' decks near their final draws. If you've counted the cards accurately, you know what final cards remain. Time to bet big. *Beat the Dealer* became a must-read classic. Interest in the game spiked, putting the fear of card-counters in the minds every casino boss, and eventually changing some of the house rules too.

In 1980, a group of MIT students put Professor Thorp's theory into practice, first in Atlantic City, and then in Las Vegas. Gamblers try to count cards all the time, but few can concentrate for very long. The

Liza Lapira and Kate Bosworth in the 2008 film *21*, about the MIT Blackjack Team

initial MIT Blackjack Team was composed of 10 science-minded students who remained focused on the task. Their coordinated efforts earned profits of nearly $200 per hour in their first tries. For nearly 15 years, members came and went, their escapades unnoticed, reaping millions of dollars in winnings.

Coached by a former professor in Cambridge, Massachusetts, the team mastered subtle cues: a comment about a stool might be a reference to a three, the number of legs on the stool. A sign could be as simple as stroking one's hair, indicating that the main player should stay away a little longer. They developed a training methodology, recruited more students and even wrote a software program to analyze their strategies.

At the casino, each member played a specific role. Some were card players while others provided support. If a card count indicated that the rest of the deck was in favor of the house, a player might step out to the washroom. When that player returned, non-verbal cues from another member of the team who was still counting determined if the player should stick around or not. By betting only when the hand was advantageous, the MIT team maximized its financial returns.

Throughout the 1980s, MIT team members flew from Boston to Las Vegas for extravagant weekends, often returning with hundreds of thousands of dollars in winnings. On the long flight back to Boston, they'd prepare for the reality of Monday-morning college exams.

By the early 1990s, Professor Thorp's theory had been proven spectacularly time and again. The experienced MIT players were so sure of the cards that they grew cocky, betting tens of thousands of dollars on a single blackjack hand. That got them noticed. Casinos like big spenders because they lose big too. That's why high rollers are offered complimentary hotel rooms, dinners and transportation: Casinos assume that all players eventually lose more than they win. The MIT Blackjack Team took full advantage of the perks offered and just kept on winning. Casinos were always on the lookout for individual hustlers, but remained unaware of the organized team.

By 1994, success went to those brainy MIT heads. The earliest players had kept quiet about their wealth, but the newest members were conspicuous, accepting more than just free flights to Las Vegas. They received tickets to the biggest boxing matches and the most popular stage shows, plus VIP treatment in their free hotel rooms at places like The Mirage, MGM Grand and Caesars Palace. But there was one critical factor that their trainer failed to consider: security at competing resorts talk to each other, comparing observations about the clientele. The casino's detectives started to recognize certain patterns of friends.

Since the publication of Thorp's book, casino bosses were on the lookout for card counters breaking the rules. But only *individual* card counters, who were sometimes caught and then barred from future play. Eventually, the casinos' detectives noticed the high concentration of barred players from Cambridge, Massachusetts. When casino detectives matched photos from college yearbooks against the photographs in their image database, the MIT Blackjack Team was exposed.

The bust made news among casinos around the world. Team members were banned forever from every club in Las Vegas and in many resorts around the world. The long winning streak for the MIT Blackjack Team ended unceremoniously. Today, players caught counting cards at blackjack tables in Las Vegas are asked to leave the game.

The Blackjack Team that was busted in 1994 lives on in the media. Author Ben Mezrich documented the exploits of the final MIT team in his best-selling book *Bringing Down the House* in 2002, explaining how they achieved their spectacular wealth and provoked their own downfall. The book was made into the feature film *21*, released in 2008, starring Kevin Spacey as the professor and Laurence Fishburne as the detective who breaks the case.

Professor Thorp's *Beat the Dealer* sold over a half-million copies. In the 21st century, it is still considered an industry standard among gamblers, hailed as the book that changed the rules in Las Vegas.

1 The Mirage: 3400 S. Las Vegas Blvd.
2 MGM Grand: 3799 Las Vegas Blvd. S.
3 Caesars Palace: 3570 Las Vegas Blvd. S.

■ Existing Building
■ Building No Longer Exists

CHAPTER 27.

THE ENTREPRENEUR

Large corporations own most resorts in Las Vegas, with one notable exception.

Entrepreneur Steve Wynn is responsible for much of the expansion on the Strip. As the past or present owner of the Golden Nugget, Mirage, Treasure Island, Bellagio, Wynn and Encore, he's also a billionaire.

Wynn's father Michael ran a string of bingo parlors on the East Coast. In 1963, he died just weeks before his son's graduation from the University of Pennsylvania. With a B.A. in English Lit, young Steve Wynn inherited a company, plus his father's $350,000 gambling debt.

Wynn reorganized the company, running the family's bingo operation in Maryland. Things went so well that four years later he traded in the bingo enterprise for a minority stake in the Frontier Hotel and Casino, relocating to Las Vegas with his wife in 1967. "One thing my father's gambling debt showed me at a very early age was that to make money in a casino…the answer is to own one," he explained.

The Wynn Las Vegas and Encore, two resorts by Steve Wynn

At age 29, Steve Wynn bought a parking lot adjacent to Caesars Palace from Howard Hughes for $1.1 million. When the owners at Caesars learned that Wynn might open a competing casino on the lot, they paid him $2.25 million for it. He used that money to buy a majority stake in the Golden Nugget, one of the most neglected casinos downtown. Wynn's aim was to turn the gambling hall into Fremont Street's first resort hotel and casino.

On a tip from a bartender at another casino, Wynn put a stop to the ongoing theft at the Golden Nugget, confronting employees who met in the bar at 4 a.m. daily to divide their share of a skim. He gave the place a much-needed facelift, reinventing one of the oldest downtown saloons in the process. Within a year, the Golden Nugget's profits quadrupled to over $4 million. By 1977, after Wynn added a hotel tower, profits reportedly jumped to $12 million.

The renovated Golden Nugget was the classiest act on Fremont Street; Steve Wynn was a multi-millionaire at age 35.

When New Jersey voters legalized gambling in Atlantic City in 1976, Las Vegas faced its first rival on American soil. Wynn envisioned an East Coast expansion for the Golden Nugget. He bought in early, acquiring an old motel on the Boardwalk for $8.5 million; then he tore it down and built a 500-room hotel and casino for $140 million.

At the Golden Nugget Atlantic City, Wynn and Wall Street investment banker Michael Milken reinvented the business model for financing a casino. Most of the construction costs were financed through high-risk bonds offered by Milken's investment bank. Wynn didn't need to solicit cash from organized crime or the Teamsters Union, and he didn't finance it out of his own pocket. He'd learned to make wise use of other people's money. Milken became Wynn's partner in New Jersey. The Golden Nugget Atlantic City opened in 1980, owned by Golden Nugget Enterprises and Michael R. Milken. With its crystal chandeliers, stained glass and vaulted ceilings, it was the most profitable casino in town, even though it was one of the smallest.

In 1987, Milken and Wynn proved to be well positioned when a power struggle erupted in Atlantic City. When the owners of Bally's offered $440 million for the casino—twice its estimated value—the partners promptly cashed out, then brought their profits back to Las Vegas.

Their next venture would reinvent the Las Vegas Strip. In 1989, Wynn opened the Mirage, his opulent new resort and casino that welcomed a new kind of customers: families. With an indoor forest, a 20,000-gallon aquarium and an outdoor "volcano," the Mirage was a family-friendly entertainment oasis in the middle of Sin City. No snarky comics or Rat Pack shows for grownups here; the theater at the Mirage featured Siegfried and Roy, a dazzling mini-circus that appealed to all ages. Wynn was involved in everything, including design and construction.

The $630 million construction was financed mainly with junk bonds issued by Milken. Months later, Milken was indicted on 98 counts of securities fraud, caught by a federal insider trading investigation. His felonies were a scandal on Wall Street in 1989. With a plea bargain that included fines and restitution, Milken was sentenced to 10 years in prison but was released after serving two. (With a net worth of about $2 billion in 2010, Milken is still one of the 500 wealthiest individuals on earth.) Milken and his junk bonds were no longer a source of capital for Wynn's Las Vegas endeavors.

But Wynn didn't need them. He anticipated that there might be 100 players on earth who would gamble with as much as $1 million. Six weeks after the Mirage opened, Wynn's office printed a list of gamblers who had bet more than $1 million. The list ran for 20 pages: 400 names! Milken was in jail, but Wynn had no shortage of potential investors.

The numbers crunchers at competing corporations were stunned by Wynn's success. They calculated that his 3,000-room enterprise would require $1 million a day just to meet expenses. They scoffed that the ratio of staff to guests was too high to be profitable, but Wynn proved them wrong. The Mirage was profitable from its very first month. At the end of its first year of operation, the enormous hotel averaged a whopping 90 percent occupancy rate.

Property owners along the Strip took action. They raced to mimic the theme park concept, toppling the Strip's first generation of luxury hotels in the process. The Sands, the Dunes, the Aladdin, the Landmark, the Stardust and the New Frontier were demolished, to be replaced by fantasy resorts on a grand scale. Wynn's competitors soon included resorts with roller coasters and singing gondoliers.

Treasure Island Hotel and Casino was Wynn's next fantasy project, built on the property adjacent to the Mirage in 1993. To continue his success with the family market, Wynn built the Strip's first mini-theme park. At

STEVE WYNN AND THE PICASSO

For decades, Steve Wynn invested in valuable paintings. Some decorate his properties, some are loaned to museums, and many remain in his private collection.

In 2001, Wynn bought a painting called *Le Rêve* (*The Dream*) by Pablo Picasso. He paid an Austrian-born collector an undisclosed sum, estimated to be about $60 million.

The vibrant colors in *Le Rêve* served as Wynn's palette for the décor at the Wynn Las Vegas resort; the hotel was even called *Le Rêve* during its construction phase. Months after the hotel's grand opening, Wynn agreed to sell the painting for $139 million. It would have set a record as the highest price ever paid for a single work of art.

Fate intervened. Afflicted with retinitis pigmentosa, a degenerative eye disease, Wynn accidentally put his elbow through the multi-million dollar canvas while showing it to newscaster Barbara Walters and other guests. The deal was off.

Wynn paid $90,000 for a meticulous repair to Picasso's painting, but following the repair, the painting's value was reduced to $85 million. Though it now has a colorful history, to knowledgeable collectors, Picasso's *Le Rêve* will always be damaged goods.

Treasure Island, the entertainment began when guests walked a gangplank to reach the hotel's front door. A pirate show was performed at the front entrance for free several times a day. Buccaneer Bay was the freshest attraction on the Strip. Inside, Cirque du Soleil made its debut. Like Siegfried and Roy at the Mirage, *Mystère* was another fun-for-all-ages success.

Next, Wynn bought the Dunes and demolished it. In its place, he erected the most expensive hotel on earth, the Bellagio, at a cost of $1.6 billion. When it opened in October 1998, it was proclaimed as one of the most beautiful hotels in the world. Inspired by the serene village of Bellagio, Italy, which overlooks Lake Como, the resort overlooks an eight-acre fountain with its popular Dancing Waters show. The theme continues inside, where Wynn built a special theater to accommodate Cirque du Soleil's aquatic circus, staged in 1.5 million gallons of water.

Less than two years after the Bellagio's opening, Wynn lost control of Mirage Resorts in a hostile takeover by Kirk Kerkorian at the MGM Grand. When the two firms

→ The Dunes hotel in the 1950s, and the resort that replaced it in 1998, the Bellagio

merged in June 2000, $6.6 billion was paid for control of the Mirage properties. The sale enhanced Wynn's standing as one of the wealthiest men on earth, but he no longer commanded the dynasty he built. He paid for the flaw in Milken's original strategy: since the origins of the company were built with other people's money, Wynn didn't hold a controlling interest in his company. Kerkorian bought up sufficient shares from Wynn's investors, then pounced.

It didn't take long for Wynn to rebound. Weeks before the Mirage deal closed, he bought the Desert Inn, former home to Howard Hughes. In 2001, he imploded it and built a luxurious resort called the Wynn, which opened in 2005. He followed it with a second tower named Encore in 2008, this time with a controlling interest in the stock, reducing the risk of another hostile takeover.

In 2006, *Time* magazine included Wynn as one of the World's 100 Most Influential People. Later that year, he was inducted in the American Gaming Association Hall of Fame.

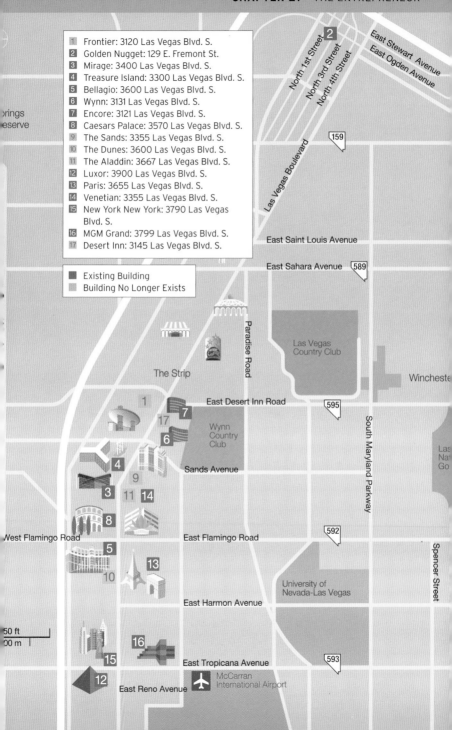

1. Frontier: 3120 Las Vegas Blvd. S.
2. Golden Nugget: 129 E. Fremont St.
3. Mirage: 3400 Las Vegas Blvd. S.
4. Treasure Island: 3300 Las Vegas Blvd. S.
5. Bellagio: 3600 Las Vegas Blvd. S.
6. Wynn: 3131 Las Vegas Blvd. S.
7. Encore: 3121 Las Vegas Blvd. S.
8. Caesars Palace: 3570 Las Vegas Blvd. S.
9. The Sands: 3355 Las Vegas Blvd. S.
10. The Dunes: 3600 Las Vegas Blvd. S.
11. The Aladdin: 3667 Las Vegas Blvd. S.
12. Luxor: 3900 Las Vegas Blvd. S.
13. Paris: 3655 Las Vegas Blvd. S.
14. Venetian: 3355 Las Vegas Blvd. S.
15. New York New York: 3790 Las Vegas Blvd. S.
16. MGM Grand: 3799 Las Vegas Blvd. S.
17. Desert Inn: 3145 Las Vegas Blvd. S.

Existing Building
Building No Longer Exists

CHAPTER 28.

HOUSE OF CARDS

For over a decade starting in 1990, Las Vegas was the fastest growing city in America, a place where workers could earn comfortable wages even if they lacked college degrees. Employment wasn't limited to the hospitality and gaming industries either, since many professions are needed to run a thriving metropolis in the desert. In the decade between 1990 and 2000, the city's population swelled by a whopping 85 percent, making Las Vegas America's 28th largest city, with nearly half a million residents.

During the decade of Bill Clinton's presidency, hoteliers reinvented Las Vegas as an adult fantasyland. The last of Howard Hughes's hotels were imploded so that giddy architectural feats could burst upon Las Vegas Boulevard practically every year: a Sphinx and a pyramid, a crenellated fortress, a mini-Eiffel Tower, a reduction of the Manhattan skyline. The city government responded with equal enthusiasm. It built schools and roads and hospitals for its residents, and four skywalks over Las Vegas Boulevard to help visitors explore the new resorts. In 1994, the Fremont Street Experience was inaugurated: a lightshow on a canopy running the

← The Fremont Street Experience

The new CityCenter complex

entire length of downtown's first boulevard. Construction began on a Town Center: a sprawling commercial and residential expansion to the west, near Red Rock.

In Nevada, famous for its low taxes, the state and city governments were supported by a 12 percent Resort Tax collected at all casinos. As large-scale conventions flocked to the Strip's resorts, regularly filling those 3,000-room hotels, Nevada's coffers were replenished.

When the nation's economy took a dip following the terrorist attacks on September 11, 2001, the Las Vegas economy was comparatively quick to recover. During the years of George W. Bush's presidency, the hospitality industry saw year-over-year increases in visitors and revenue. Developers became convinced of Las Vegas's invincibility. They began to take the place seriously, designing upscale resorts devoid of 1990s whimsy. In place of theme park fantasies, urban high-rises asserted a newfound sophistication on the Las Vegas Strip.

These sober new residences were pitched to attract the world's high rollers. In 2005, Donald Trump was one of the first developers to break ground on a high-end Las Vegas condominium. He planned to sell 1,282 units in a 64-story monolith sheathed in gold-infused glass, even promoting its development on his TV show. He was not alone in anticipating that some steady gamblers would prefer to own an apartment above the Strip in lieu of a rented hotel room above a smoky casino.

Weeks later, in October 2005, the Cosmopolitan broke ground beside the enormously successful Bellagio, with 2,200 condominium-hotel units and 800 hotel rooms planned. Trumping them both, however, was Kirk Kerkorian at the MGM Grand, with Dubai World as his financing partner. On 76 acres in the middle of the Las Vegas Strip, MGM and Dubai World broke ground on City Center in June 2006, the largest privately funded construction project in American history. The $9 billion complex was planned as 2,400 condominium apartments and 4,800 hotel rooms spread across six buildings. The square footage surpassed the size of the original Rockefeller Center in Manhattan.

When construction commenced on these three high-profile projects, new investors imitated the same business model: sell condominium units from blueprints to finance the construction, then upon completion, collect steady income from hotel suites that were essentially financed by the condo purchasers.

ELAD Properties, the owners of the Plaza Hotel in New York City, set a new record for land acquisition on the Strip, paying over $33 million per acre to acquire the New Frontier hotel just to demolish it. In its place, the firm planned the Plaza Las Vegas: 2,600 condominium apartments on 34 acres, spread over seven buildings that copied the design elements of Manhattan's most famous hotel façade.

In April 2007, the Fontainebleau broke ground, planned as a cousin to the famous Miami Beach resort, featuring 1,018 condominium units on a 24-acre expanse formerly occupied by the historic El Rancho hotel.

Rejecting the condo/hotel business model, Boyd Gaming Corp. demolished the famous old Stardust Hotel in 2007 to build Echelon Place: 5,300 hotel rooms spread over 87 acres in four buildings, plus a one-million-square-foot convention center.

None of these developers had a chance to test that business model because in March 2008, with the projects nearing completion, investment bank Bear Stearns collapsed, a prelude to Wall Street's impending disaster. Two weeks later, Donald Trump soldiered on, opening Trump International Hotel Las Vegas with predictable fanfare but barely one quarter of the units sold. Then, on September 29, 2008, the Dow Jones Industrial Average plummeted 778 points. When President Bush exclaimed, "This sucker is going down," the American economy crapped out.

Disposable income vanished. Corporations tightened their belts. Those large-scale conventions in Las Vegas were recalled sentimentally as a relic of the bygone Clinton era. Low occupancy rates in the hotels meant a drastic reduction in Resort Taxes, punishing the state's coffers. Development plummeted. The once-fastest growing city became the place with the highest foreclosure rate in the nation. Within weeks of Wall Street's collapse, Nevada was burdened with the highest unemployment rate in America, a number which eventually rose to 15 percent.

Builders of the Las Vegas construction projects were frantic. MGM restructured the deal with its Dubai investors, a gutsy move to complete the mammoth City Center. It opened as planned in December 2009, more hotel than condo. The Cosmopolitan abandoned its marketing plan for condo sales and opened as a 2,995-room hotel the following year instead.

The Cosmopolitan was the only hotel to open on the Strip in 2010, since other developers showed less spleen. ELAD postponed construction of the Plaza Las Vegas indefinitely. The site at 3120 Las Vegas Boulevard South and Desert Inn Road is a vacant lot, no longer worth $33 million per acre. The Fontainebleau was forced to halt construction when it was 70 percent complete. Bank of America, the resort's primary lender, refused to provide financing on its committed line of credit, forcing the resort's operator into bankruptcy. The site at 2500 Las Vegas Boulevard South near Sahara Avenue looms quiet, with no prospects for its completion. Echelon Place at 3300 Las Vegas Boulevard South near Riviera Boulevard has become the largest eyesore in Las Vegas: 87 acres of partially-constructed concrete and steel oxidizing in the desert sun. There are no plans to resume construction.

To many, eras are remembered not by their dates, but by the milestone events that frame them. Las Vegas in 1999 may be remembered at one of its headiest peaks: unencumbered by gangsters, with tourism and construction on the rise, an urban environment thriving in the desert. But, after years of unregulated investment speculation, the millennial decade came to a close with brutal finality. Even the trains that once put Las Vegas on the map no longer stop here. What lies beyond the milestone is uncertain, but an era has ended.

For Las Vegas, the next chapter awaits.

1 Fremont Street Experience: Fremont Street from
   Main Street to Las Vegas Boulevard South
2 Trump Las Vegas: 2000 Fashion Show Drive
3 The Cosmopolitan: 3708 Las Vegas Blvd. S.
4 CityCenter: 3780 Las Vegas Blvd. S.
5 Plaza Las Vegas Site: 3120 Las Vegas Blvd. S.
6 Fontainebleau Site: 2500 Las Vegas Blvd. S.
7 Echelon Place Site: 3000 Las Vegas Blvd. S.

Existing Building
Building No Longer Exists

CHAPTER 29.

BRIEF HISTORY OF GAMBLING

Ancient people in Mesopotamia believed that spirits determined the outcome when dice were rolled. The Romans elevated gambling into a spectacle, betting on chariot races and gladiator matches in action-packed arenas. By the time Christopher Columbus set sail for the New World, there were over 100 popular betting games played across Europe by nobles and peasants alike.

In 21st-century Las Vegas, that list is reduced considerably; most casinos offer between 20 and 30 casino games with origins from many cultures.

DICE

Probably the oldest of all games, dice were developed independently by several ancient cultures. Ancient Greeks gambled with dice made from the knucklebones of sheep, and gamblers have "rolled them bones" ever since. In Arabia today, the word for dice is the same word used for knucklebones.

In ancient Egypt, ornately carved ivory dice were installed among the treasures with the pharaohs. Dice recovered from some Egyptian tombs date back to 2000 BCE and earlier. The oldest known dice were unearthed in the 20th century, part of a 5,000-year old backgammon set excavated at Shahr-i Sokhta, the Burnt City, in southeastern Iran.

To the ancient Romans, a roll of the bones delivered a message from Fortuna, revered as the goddess of luck who determined its outcome. Entrusting fates to Fortuna, ancient people cast their dice to divide inheritances, choose rulers and determine their futures. Professional gamblers were common in ancient Rome; some of the first written laws in civilization were passed by the Roman Senate to define the legalities of tossing the dice. (For starters: if you allow gambling in your house, you can't press charges if you're swindled or assaulted.)

Dice evolved in appearance; some ancient dice have as many as 20 faceted sides. New games were devised: the Chinese invented dominoes from all the combinations on a pair of dice. During the Crusades, medieval knights wagered on dice games to pass the time as they blockaded castles.

In England, the popular game of Hazard is believed to have originated as far back as 1125. When America's earliest settlers brought their knowledge of that English dice game to the New World in the 1600s, the Puritan leaders at Plymouth Colony admonished them. In 1656, several laws were passed to prohibit gambling. Punishment for the first offense was a fine; additional offenses were punished by public whipping.

A century later, Thomas Jefferson spoke for many Americans when he warned that gambling "corrupts our dispositions, and teaches us a habit of hostility against all mankind." In puritanical America, gambling was viewed as an irresponsible risk: money should be used to feed and shelter your family instead. The common adage was: "The best throw of the dice is to throw the dice away."

But dice games were impossible to suppress. They were too easy to make. Committed players simply devised new methods to circumvent the existing laws. Roughly 735 riverboats paddled America's waterways between 1820 and 1860. They were floating casinos, where more than 2,000 professional gamblers earned their living. Dry land had its dice games too, illegal, but numerous. Hundreds of tents with sawdust floors were pitched along the Barbary Coast, San Francisco's waterfront in 1855. Dice games were offered 24 hours a day.

Since 1931, when Nevada legalized the wagers on dice games, most professional gamblers agree: Dice games offer the best odds in the casino...but only if you make the right bets.

CRAPS

Craps is the most popular dice game in today's casinos, where one player rolls the dice while everyone else at the table bets on the outcome of the roll. Craps is descended from the British game of Hazard. The name "Craps" is derived from "Crabs," the term for the lowest roll in a Hazard game. (Americans call it "Snake Eyes.")

French settlers brought their version of Craps to New Orleans around 1800. Its first mention in America occurred in 1804, when the wealthy planter Bernard de Marigny lost so much money in a Craps game that he was forced to sell his land. When the property was divided, he named one street the Rue de Craps. (It's Burgundy Street in today's New Orleans.) With the advent of riverboat gamblers in the 1800s, Craps became the most popular game along the Mississippi River.

Crooked dice were a problem, making many American gamblers wary of the game. Then, dicemaker John H. Winn revised the rules in the 19th century to satisfy the skeptics. The improvement: in Winn's game,

Roulette players in a Reno casino, 1910

players could bet *against* the shooter in addition to the usual rule of accepting what was tossed. Winn also added the "Pass" and "Don't Pass" lines that are standard on craps tables everywhere today.

It was African-American roustabouts working along the Mississippi River who took the Craps game beyond the river towns. Craps became a common game among soldiers; by the close of World War II, it was the most popular casino game in Las Vegas.

ROULETTE

During the French Revolution, as emotions ran high, the number of Frenchmen willing to gamble reached new heights as well. Gaming was popular among all social strata, from peasants to aristocrats. Many of the dice and card games played in Las Vegas today have their origins in 1790s France.

That includes Roulette, which made its entrance during the French Revolution at the casino in Paris's Palais Royale. It combined three British wheel games into one.

Roly-Poly, sometimes called Rowlet, was a popular betting game in England. Gamblers placed their wagers on a number, then a marble rolled around a horizontal wheel with numbered slots. Two slots were reserved for the house. Gamblers won when the ball landed on their number or lost if the ball lodged in one of the two slots for the house.

Ace of Hearts was another game that involved a horizontal wheel and a spinning marble. Gamblers placed their bets on a card table where corresponding cards were painted on the wheel.

A third wheel game was Evens/Odds, or E/O. It involved a spinning wheel with 40 slots. Half were even, half were odd, except for the two profitable slots that went to the bank. The game was popular because the almost-50/50 odds were so favorable.

The Palais Royale game combined all three features to devise the Roulette we play today: the table is similar to Ace of Hearts, but arrayed with 36 numbers instead of cards. It includes a section for Even/Odd bets, plus bets for individual numbers, as in Roly-Poly. The original French game had both zero and double zero marked in green on the board and the wheel.

To compete among European casinos, the spa in Homburg, Germany, introduced a Roulette wheel with just one green zero slot. Better odds for players, reduced returns for the house. When the German government abolished gambling in the 1860s, German Roulette moved to the last legal casino in Europe: Monte Carlo. The casinos in Monaco became gambling hubs for European elite, where a spinning Roulette wheel was one of Monte Carlo's most alluring attractions. The single zero slot became the new European standard.

Gamblers playing the card game faro in a Reno casino, 1910

However, Roulette came to America before that, when the French settled New Orleans. Their wheel featured two green zero slots, guaranteeing a greater profit for the house. The French double zero made its way up the Mississippi on riverboats, establishing two green slots as the American standard played in Las Vegas today.

CARDS

For millennia, dice games reigned as the favorite pastime among gamblers. Then, some time after the fall of Rome, playing cards were conceived by several cultures.

Since cards weren't built to last, it's difficult for researchers to determine exactly which civilization played them first. The earliest evidence points to India, where the noble classes were amused by round, hand-painted cards made of ivory, mother-of-pearl and wood. Around the year 900, Chinese gamblers devised a paper version of dominoes. The first known deck of rectangular playing cards is a Chinese domino deck representing each of the 21 dice combinations. (It also served as the genesis for mah-jongg tiles.)

Saracens introduced cards to Europeans in the Middle Ages. The earliest decks featured four suits from the tarot: cups, wands, swords and pentacles. By 1370, card games were popular across Europe, but they remained playthings for the rich because hand-painted playing cards were prohibitively expensive.

Then, around 1400, woodblock prints reduced the cost and increased exposure; about 50 years later, stencils brought sophistication to mass production. Soon, cards were available to people of all social strata.

How many cards are in a deck? No one agreed. The four suits we know today, hearts, diamonds, spades and clubs, originated in France around 1480. The tarot cards evolved: pentacles became diamonds, wands became clubs, cups became hearts and swords became spades. A French deck had 56 cards, including a king, queen, knight and knave. Other Europeans eliminated the queens completely. In some German decks, queens replaced kings as the highest card. Then, in the late 18th century, another radical idea emerged from France. In the years leading up to the French Revolution, the ace, the lowest card, was elevated to *overtake* the king. In "aces high" games, the commoners symbolically rose above the aristocrats. Card-players in America, recently winning independence from British monarchs, followed their lead, as did much of Europe. (Then the French eliminated *all* kings and queens from the deck but nobody followed their lead, so with the rise of Napoleon in 1805, French decks conformed again.)

What did Americans contribute? The Joker. In Colonial America, where life was hard and entertainment scarce, cards were a welcome amusement. The founding fathers, like much of the population, played Euchre, a game in which the Joker is the secret card that trumps all others.

Today, it's the cards themselves that trump all others. While Craps, a dice game, once reigned as the most popular casino game, cards now attract the most gamblers in Las Vegas. When aces are high, commoners continue to overtake aristocrats.

BLACKJACK

Blackjack is descended from the French game Vingt-et-Un, or Twenty-One, a game that appeared in French casinos around 1700. Players draw cards trying to total as close to 21 as possible without going over. To win, the player's sum must be closer to 21 than the sum of the cards drawn by the dealer.

The difference between Twenty-One and Blackjack: in Twenty-One, only the dealer may double the wager when dealt two 10- or 11-point cards.

When Nevada first legalized gambling in 1931, the game was still called Twenty-One. Some casinos offered a special bet to attract a crowd: They'd pay 10 times the wager to anyone who drew the Ace of Spades plus a jack from either of the black suits, clubs or spades. That's how the combination earned its moniker: Blackjack. (Casinos ended the big payout long ago.) In today's Las Vegas, Blackjack refers to the combination of any ace plus a 10 or face card, regardless of suit.

POKER

Poker, often called America's national card game, has a polyglot history. The variety of poker games offered in Las Vegas today are uniquely

American versions of Poque, a French game from the 1700s. Poque is a variation of Pochen, a German game that literally means "to bluff," and Pochen is descended from Primero in Spain and Primiera in Italy, that date back to the Renaissance. In all these games, players bet and bluff on the combinations of the cards they are dealt; they're the predecessors to both Poker and Bridge.

When French settlers brought Poque to New Orleans in the early 1800s, the American drawl soon turned it into Poker. Prior to the Civil War, when the West was being settled, Americans added a new twist that changed the game. Instead of betting on the hand one is dealt, the Draw was introduced: players discard the cards they don't want, hoping to replace them with better ones. This addition embodied the American spirit, especially out West, where many Americans went to start over.

The game continued to evolve in America, which explains its multiple versions in casinos today. The most recent addition, the concept of "community cards" arrived around 1925. In this American variation, notably Texas Hold 'Em, all players share cards dealt face up on the table. Each player is dealt a private, incomplete hand, then utilizes the community cards to make a winning combination.

Poker terms have become an intrinsic part of American culture, turning up frequently in everyday conversation. An *ace up one's sleeve, beats me, call one's bluff, ace in the hole, poker face,* are all terms that originated at America's card tables.

CHAPTER 30.

THE FIRST SPIN: SLOT MACHINES

Quick: What's the most popular attraction in a Las Vegas casino? Blackjack? Craps? No, it's America's contribution to gaming: the Slot Machine.

More people play the slots than any table game in a Las Vegas casino. On many nights, that means the house reaps its biggest profits from the slots as well.

The first machines were invented during the industrial revolution, shortly before Las Vegas was founded. In the 1890s, mechanical gadgets were popping up everywhere. Phonographs, light bulbs, Oldsmobiles and telephones: technology was reinventing popular culture. Even children's savings banks were mechanical.

What if some of those mechanical banks occasionally returned a few coins? Insert a nickel and take a chance that it might dispense more nickels in return. Coin-operated devices became a popular novelty on

Slot machines in a Las Vegas casino

the Barbary Coast, San Francisco's rowdy district of booze, dice and prostitutes. The earliest gambling machines were made back East, but the best "nickel-in-the-slot machines" were manufactured by two local vendors.

In 1892, Gustav Schultze patented a mechanical wheel with 25 stripes that he called *Horseshoes*, the first gaming device with an automatic payout dispenser. Put your nickel in the slot, watch the wheel spin, and hope that it lands on one of the 10 stripes marked with a horseshoe. They rewarded 10 cents or 25 cents to the gambler, paid directly from the machine, not a nearby attendant. Another stripe was the Joker, good for a free drink. The other 14 slots depicted stars and cards, but no payout. Take your chance.

Nickel-in-the-slot-machines gained popularity immediately across San Francisco, with mechanical devices in every saloon and cigar store. On July 10, 1893, the *San Francisco Chronicle* reported that there were "1,500 nickel-in-the-slot-machines in the city, this number mushrooming rapidly, all doing good business, taking enormous profits." (Incidentally, a nickel wasn't exactly pocket change in 1893. It's worth about $1.25 in 2010.)

Schultze soon partnered with Charles August Fey to make a line of automatic payout machines during the 1890s. They were clever, mechanical devices that sat on a bar or a retail counter; some machines even doled out cigars to the winners instead of coins. The partners didn't sell the machines; they leased them for up to $40 per year. The only way a competitor could duplicate Schultze and Fey's ingenuity would be to steal one.

In their factory at 406 Market Street, Fey had a stroke of genius that earned him recognition as the father of the modern slot machine: he introduced *suspense*. Instead of spinning one wheel, spin three, like reels side-by-side. Reward certain combinations after the first, second and third reels stopped spinning in succession. Fey patented his Card Bell in 1898.

The machine's reels were set in motion when a gambler inserted a nickel and pulled down on the cast-iron handle. When the reels stopped spinning, automatic payouts ranged from two to twenty coins, or none, depending upon the alignment of playing cards depicted on the reels. The highest payout went to a simulated royal flush: ace, king and queen in one suit.

ONE-ARMED BANDIT

Unlike today's slots, early mechanical slot machines didn't use electricity. When the player inserted a coin and pulled down on the handle, the machine's "one-arm," that yank set the three reels spinning.

The slot machine gained its reputation as a "one-armed bandit" for a sleazy reason. Since the machines were all mechanical, it wasn't that difficult for unethical casino bosses to tamper with the hardware inside. By attaching a "bug," a small piece of metal, onto the gear that determined where the final reel would stop, they forced the reel always to bypass a specific spot. A slot machine might never hit its big jackpot because a bug made sure that the winning combination never fell into place. Unwitting players thought they had at least a small chance of winning the jackpot, when in fact they had none. They were fleeced by a one-armed bandit.

The house pocketed that extra money, usually earmarked as the skim paid to organized crime, or as a payoff to politicians and police. Attorney General Robert F. Kennedy discovered evidence of tampered slot machines during his investigations in the 1960s, but at about the same time, Bally's introduced the first electrified slot machines, devices too complex for such obvious tampering. The new machines deterred the corruption identified by Kennedy and his investigators.

Although the arm was no longer needed to put the wheels in spin on Bally's electrified slot machines, some new machines kept the arm just for its familiarity. Today's slot machines play a faster game since players press a button instead. And, today's machines process many more combinations than their mechanical forebears. By Nevada law, each machine must pay a minimum of 75 percent of its income back to the players. Thanks to computer chips, the machine can withhold that payout far longer than its mechanical forebears, eventually bestowing newsworthy jackpots.

Playing many rounds while waiting to hit that jackpot may be one reason why players haven't forgotten the term "one-armed bandit."

The following year, the partners topped the Card Bell's success by adding a Liberty Bell image to each reel. Trumping the playing card combinations, if a player's nickel aligned all three Liberty Bells, the machine dispensed a token, redeemable for up to two dollars from the hosting establishment, usually drinks or cigars. The concept of the "jackpot" was born. The Liberty Bell, patented in 1899, was the partnership's last — and biggest — success.

In 1905, a Liberty Bell was stolen from a Powell Street saloon. A year later, it surfaced at the Mills Novelty plant (then in Chicago, Illinois), a firm that was soon mass-producing Liberty Bell machines. Caille Brothers in Detroit knocked them off too. Before Schultze and Fey could pursue the pirates, the tragic 1906 earthquake and fire decimated San Francisco. Their business lay in shambles. The Market Street factory and its contents were lost.

Schultze and Fey made over 100 Liberty Bells; now their competitors flooded the market with hundreds more, sold by mail order catalogs to bars and bowling alleys every year. An industry was born. Cheap knock-offs sold for $40 apiece; ornate new cabinets designed to stand on the floor sold for $50 to $125. For much of the 20th century, the term "Bell" was casino parlance for a three-reel slot machine.

The popularity of the machines spread beyond San Francisco's Barbary Coast to the mining towns in California and nearby Nevada. Not all machines dispensed coins or cigars. Some simply generated gumballs, or tokens to be redeemed for drinks or merchandise. In the General Store, even kids could play. That aroused detractors.

Slot machines were a "vice." Reformers, clergymen and women's clubs decried the $12 million in "lost wages" that went into San Francisco's 3,200 slot machines. Although the Wells Fargo Bank warned of an economic meltdown, the San Francisco Board of Supervisors banned slot machines in 1909. One-fifth of the city's cigar stores promptly went broke, since they relied on the steady income from their slot machines. Unfazed, California's governor expanded the law, signing a bill in 1911 that made slot machines illegal across the entire state.

That was Nevada's cue. Slot machines had been illegal for a brief time, but in 1912, Nevada's state legislature began to license nickel-in-the-slot machines, restricting them to social games that paid out cigars or drinks, not cash. Mills Novelty Company devised new machines with the images of fruits on its reels. It dispensed fruit-flavored chewing gum according to the images that aligned, familiar symbols still in use on slot machines today.

When Nevada legalized gambling in 1931, slot machines resumed their cash payouts. They also filled the state coffers during the toughest years of the Great Depression: Nevada collected licensing fees of $10 per slot per month. The first slot machines licensed for gambling in Las Vegas could be found at the Meadows, Tony Cornero's casino on Fremont Street. When the Hoover Dam workers arrived on payday, Cornero's five slot machines couldn't possibly accommodate the demand. (Cornero installed 120 slot machines on the *S.S. Rex*, his gambling ship in international waters beyond the state's jurisdiction.) During the Great Depression, Nevada maintained one of America's most stable economies, thanks in part to the revenue generated from scores of slot machines licensed to the new casinos in Las Vegas.

It was welcome news to inventors like Schultze (now in Oakland) and to competitors like Fey and Mills (both in San Francisco now). They created a dazzling, and seemingly infinite variety of mechanical devices. Over the next decades, new slots would also play music, vend cigarettes, tell your fortune—the Futurity game even guaranteed you'd win within 10 pulls. Fey invented a machine that took silver dollars. The industry was so lucrative that Illinois changed its laws to permit Bally's of Chicago to manufacture a product that was illegal in Chicago.

Bally's revolutionized slot machines. In 1963, the firm best known for its pinball machine, the Ballyhoo, devised the first fully electromechanical slot machine. Without an attendant, Bally's Money Honey could pay out up to 500 coins. Since it was powered by electricity, players no longer needed to pull on a handle to put the reels in motion. They could deposit multiple coins, then play multiple games in succession, instead of inserting one coin for one spin. Further, Bally's machines could sense more than 50 different payout combinations, making possible the three- and five-line machines in use today. On a Bally's machine, there were more ways to win (or lose).

Success was immediate. By 1969, Bally's had a near-complete monopoly on slot machines in Las Vegas, as casinos gave up their mechanical devices in favor of the more profitable new technology. Early manufacturers like the Mills Novelty Company lacked the knowledge to compete, while Bally's continued to innovate. In 1980, Bally's replaced the electromechanical circuitry with a microprocessor, introducing the electronic games seen in Las Vegas casinos today. Next,

Bally's introduced its products overseas, in every country where slots operated legally. Its overseas sales were even greater than the domestic ones. Today, American slot machines are popular features in casinos everywhere.

In over a century of slot machines, one truth remains: of all the games in a casino, slot machines offer the poorest rate of return. In Craps and Roulette, some bets have nearly an even chance of paying back. Not so with slot machines, where a player never knows the odds of hitting the next jackpot. Call that the thrill of gambling; it confirms slot machines as Las Vegas's ultimate game of chance.

INDEX

BIBLIOGRAPHY

BOOKS:

Balboni, Alan, *Tony Cornero: More Sinner Than Saint*, Las Vegas Review Journal, reprinted in *The First 100*, Stephens Press, Las Vegas, 1999.

Berman, Susan, *Lady Las Vegas*, A&E Network and TV Books, Inc., New York, 1996.

Block, Lawrence, *Gangsters, Swindlers, Killers, and Thieves: the Lives and Crimes of Fifty American Villains*, Oxford University Press, New York, 2004.

Burbank, Jeff, *Las Vegas Babylon*, M. Evans and Company, Inc., New York 2005.

Demaris, Ovid and Reid, Ed, *The Green Felt Jungle*, Buccaneer Books, Cutchogue, New York, 1963.

Denton, Sally and Morris, Roger, *The Money and the Power: the Making of Las Vegas and Its Hold on America*, Vintage Books, a Division of Random House, Inc. New York, 2001.

Dunar, Andrew J., and McBride, Dennis, *Building Hoover Dam: an Oral History of the Great Depression*, University of Nevada Press, Las Vegas, 1993.

Fey, Marshall, *Slot Machines*, Liberty Belle Books, Reno, Nevada, 1994.

Fontenay, Charles L., *Estes Kefauver, a Biography*, University of Tennessee Press, Knoxville, 1980.

Geran, Trish, *Beyond the Glimmering Lights: the Pride and Perseverance of African Americans in Las Vegas*, Stephens Press, Las Vegas, Nevada, 2006.

Goldfarb, Ronald, *Perfect Villains, Imperfect Heroes: Robert F. Kennedy's War Against Organized Crime*, Random House Inc., New York 1995.

Gorman, Joseph Bruce, *Kefauver: a Political Biography*, Oxford Press, New York, 1971.

Gottdiener, M.; Collins, Claudia C.; Dickens, David R., *Las Vegas: the Social Production of an All-American City*, Blackwell Publishers Ltd., Oxford, UK, 1999.

Kaplan, James, *Frank: The Voice*, Doubleday, New York 2010.

Land, Barbara and Myrick, *A Short History of Las Vegas*, second edition, University of Nevada Press, Reno, 2004.

Liberace, *The Wonderful Private World of Liberace*, Harpers & Row, Publishers, New York, 1986.

Littlejohn, David, *The Real Las Vegas: Life Beyond the Strip*, Oxford University Press, New York, 1999.

McCracken, Robert D., *Las Vegas: The Great American Playground*, University of Nevada Press, Las Vegas, 1997.

Okada, Shannon, *Las Vegas Casino and Hotel Outlook 2010*, HVS-Las Vegas, Las Vegas, NV, 2010.

Oppenheimer, Rex M., *Miracles Happen, You Can Bet On It!*, Heritage Media Corp, San Marcos, CA, 2005.

Pyron, Darden Asbury, *Liberace: An American Boy*, University of Chicago Press, Chicago, 2000.

Schwartz, David G., *Roll the Bones: the History of Gambling*, Gotham Books, New York 2006.

Siegfried and Roy with Tapert, Annette, *Mastering the Impossible*, William Morrow and Company, Inc., New York, 1992.

Sloane, Arthur A., *Hoffa*, The MIT Press, Cambridge, Massachusetts, 1991.

Stevens, Joseph E., *Hoover Dam: an American Adventure*, University of Oklahoma Press, Norman, OK, 1988.

Stewart, Gail B., *Gambling*, Lucent Books, Inc., San Diego, CA, 2001.

Svoboda, Peter, *Beating the Casinos At Their Own Game*, Square One Publishers, Garden City Park, New York, 2001.

Thorsen, Scott, *Behind the Candelabra: My*

Life With Liberace, E.P. Dutton, New York, 1988.

Van Vechten, Ken, *Neon Nuptials: The Complete Guide to Las Vegas Weddings*, Huntington Press, Las Vegas, NV, 2005.

Weatherford, Mike, *Cult Vegas*, Huntington Press, Las Vegas, Nevada, 2001.

Whitely, Joan Burkhart, *Young Las Vegas*, Stephens Press, Las Vegas, Nevada 2005.

Wilkerson, W. R. III, *The Man Who Invented Las Vegas*, Ciro's Books, Beverly Hills, California, 2000.

Writers' Program of the Work Projects Administration, *Nevada: A Guide to the Silver State*, American Guide Series Illustrated, Binfords & Mort, Publishers, Portland, Oregon, 1940.

PERIODICALS:

Barol, Bill, "Transition: Wladziu V. Liberace", *Newsweek*, Vol. 109, February 16, 1987

"The Case of the Invisible Billionaire", *Newsweek*, December 21, 1970.

Didion, Joan, "Marrying Absurd", *Saturday Evening Post*, December 16, 1967.

Fleming, Charles, "Viva Black Vegas", *Los Angeles*, November 1999.

Friess, Steve, "The Truth About Siegfried and Roy", *The Advocate*, November 11, 2003.

Gliatto, Tom, "Up Front: Siegfried and Roy", *People Weekly*, October 20, 2003.

Green, Michelle, "Liberace: the Gilded Showman", *People Weekly*, February 16, 1987.

Henry, William A. III, "A Synonym for Glorious Excess", *Time*, Vol. 129, February 16, 1987.

"Hughes Gambles on Las Vegas", *Business Week*, September 30, 1967.

Kishi, Stephanie, "Home of Sin City's Original Sin", *Las Vegas Sun*, May 15, 2008.

Lips, Laurie, "A 'Rosie the Riveter' is Discovered", *Airport Journals*, September 2001.

Manning, Mary, "Atomic Testing Burned Its Mark", *Las Vegas Sun*, May 15, 2008.

Manning, Mary, "Siegfried and Roy: Las Vegas's Magic Duo", *Las Vegas Sun*, May 15, 2008.

Mishak, Michael J., "In Las Vegas, Trump's Tower is a Strip Sore Spot", *Los Angeles Times*, April 30, 2011.

"The MIT Blackjack Team", *CityNet Magazine*, March 17, 2003.

Mooney, Courtney, "Historic West Las Vegas", brochure published by: Historic Preservation Commission, City of Las Vegas, 2005.

Palmeri, Christopher, "The Revenge of Steve Wynn", *Business Week*, April 11, 2005.

Patterson, Floyd with Mahon, Jack, "Cassius Clay Must Be Beaten", *Sports Illustrated*, October 11, 1965.

Powers, Ashley, "Another Part of Old Las Vegas Vanishes", *Los Angeles Times*, March 12, 2011.

Prizefighting's "Million-Dollar Gates", *Time*, March 8, 1971.

"Tony Cornero Shot At Home By Gunmen", *Los Angeles Times*, vol. LXVII, February 10, 1948.

"Shootout at the Hughes Corral", *Time*, December 21, 1970.

Star, Jack, "Why Is Howard Hughes Buying Up Las Vegas?", *LOOK*, January 23, 1969.

Stein, Joel, "Steve Wynn", *Time*, April 30, 2006.

VIDEOS:

Berman, Susan; Milio, Jim; Peltier, Melissa Jo, *The Real Las Vegas: the Complete Story of America's Neon Oasis*, The History Channel, 2001.

Ferrari, Michelle, *Las Vegas: An Unconventional History*, American Experience for PBS, 2005.

IMAGE CREDITS

6: Las Vegas Sign
iStock Photo

10: Captain John, Paiute Indian, full-length portrait, standing, facing slightly right, c 1903. Photographer may have been A.A. Forbes
Miscellaneous Items in High Demand, Prints & Photographs Division, Library of Congress, LC-USZ62-107141

11: Gathering of men and women, Pahrump Valley or Ash Meadows, n.d. Della Fisk is holding the arm of Chief Tecopa
UNLV Special Collections

12: Paiute Indian group posed in front of adobe house, between 1909 and 1932
National Photo Company Collection, Prints & Photographs Division, Library of Congress, LC-USZ62-120738

13: Courtesy Springs Preserve

14: Col. John C. Fremont, Republican candidate for the President of the United States, Baker & Godwin, c 1856
Popular Graphic Arts Collection, Prints & Photographs Division, Library of Congress, LC-DIG-pga-03112

16: Brigham Young the Colonizer, the Mormon Corridor, the state of Deseret map
UNLV Special Collections

28: Martyrdom of Joseph and Hiram Smith in Carthage jail, June 27th, 1844 / G.W. Fasel pinxit ; on stone by C.G. Crehen ; print. by Nagel & Weingaertner, N.Y.
Popular Graphic Arts Collection, Prints & Photographs Division, Library of Congress, LC-DIG-pga-02259

22: Design for a Union Station, Luther Daniels Bradley, October 18, 1907
Cartoon Drawings: Swann Collection of Caricature and Cartoon, Prints & Photographs Division, Library of Congress, LC-USZ62-84052

24: Helen J. Stewart
UNLV Special Collections

28: Hotel Las Vegas, located on the west side of North Main Street near Stewart Avenue.

Charles "pop" Squires (later editor of the *Las Vegas Age*) was the Proprietor. Built in May 1905, it was torn down in March 1906.
UNLV Special Collections

32: (top) Las Vegas Drug Store, Union Pacific Railroad depot / UNLV Special Collections
(bottom) Fremont Street in Las Vegas, Nevada, before the construction of Hoover Dam, Lake Mead and legalized gambling. Ca. 1920
Courtesy Everett Collection

34-35 Las Vegas, Nevada, c 1910
Panoramic Photographs, Prints & Photographs Division, Library of Congress, LC-USZ62-137462

38: Pictured sitting at the back bar from the notorious Arizona Club of Block 16, (now installed at the Hacienda Hotel), are: (l-R): Dick Taylor, General Manager of the Hacienda; Bob Schmuck, Hacienda Assistant Manager; and Norman Yoshpa, Assistant Manager, Hacienda. (1957)
UNLV Special Collections

40: Red Rooster Night Club, 1946 (from Nevada Life, Jan. 1946, p.13)
UNLV Special Collections

44: Three construction workers putting a coat of paint on a slanted wall of riveted-steel plates on the Hoover Dam spillway, United States. Bureau of Reclamation, Between 1936 and 1946
Miscellaneous Items in High Demand, Prints & Photographs Division, Library of Congress, LC-DIG-ppmsca-17404

46: "First grocery in Boulder City" including Mr. & Mrs. W.F. Shields, Harry Buchanan, chef, April 18, 1931
UNLV Special Collections

49: Hoover Dam
Las Vegas News Bureau

52: Gambler Tony Cornero Stralla (2L) and others gambling aboard ship Lux off coast of California.
Photo by Peter Stackpole//Time Life Pictures/Getty Images

56: The Stardust
UNLV Special Collections

58: Norma Jeane Baker, future film star Marilyn Monroe (1926 - 1962), tries her hand at sand skiing on a dune, circa 1943.
Photo by Silver Screen Collection/Hulton Archive/Getty Images

60: Cupid's Wedding Chapel
iStock Photo

65: L-R: Gus Greenbaum, Moe Sedway, ?
UNLV Special Collections

70: Bugsy Siegel, bust portrait, facing front, 1951, from a photograph taken earlier
Miscellaneous Items in High Demand, Prints & Photographs Division, Library of Congress, LC-USZ62-120728

76: Flamingo Hotel
UNLV Special Collections

78: Flamingo Hotel, exterior, night view
UNLV Special Collections

82: Gangland bullets slay "Bugsie" Siegel , 1947
Miscellaneous Items in High Demand, Prints & Photographs Division, Library of Congress, LC-USZ62-120736

86: Virginia Hill, girlfriend of Las Vegas mobster Ben 'Bugsy' Siegel,' testifies before the Kefauver organized crime hearings in New York in February 1951. Hill was portrayed by Annette Bening in the 1991 film, BUGSY.
Courtesy Everett Collection

90: A mushroom cloud rises from the desert floor at the Nevada Test Site. The nuclear test, named DeBaca, was a balloon burst fired in October 1958.
U.S. Department of Energy Collection / UNLV Special Collections

92: From Operation Teapot, the "Met" shot, a tower burst fired Apr. 15, 1955.
U.S .Department of Energy Collection / UNLV Special Collections

99: Calvin Washington (far left) runs the crap game at the El Morocco Club on the Las Vegas Westside the final night before its 1954 closing; standing next to him is Cleo Johns. Clarence Ray, night manager of the club, is not pictured.

100: Group of people seated, some standing, near a bar. Probably in a club or casino in West Las Vegas. (no date- people not identified)
UNLV Special Collections

106: Portrait of Josephine Baker, Paris
Van Vechten Collection, Prints & Photographs Division, Library of Congress, LC-DIG-ppm-sca-07816

112: Nat King Cole smoking a cigarette, 1954 June 17, LooK Magazine Collection
Miscellaneous Items in High Demand, Prints & Photographs Division, Library of Congress, LC-DIG-ppmsca-1970

112: Portrait of Harry Belafonte, singing, Carl Van Vechten, 1954 Feb. 18
Van Vechten Collection, Prints & Photographs Division, Library of Congress, LC-USZ62-103726

114: Cover of LIFE from 06-20-1955 w. headline: Newest in Las Vegas: Girls at the Moulin Rouge; photo by Loomis Dean.
Photo by Loomis Dean/Life Magazine, Copyright Time Inc./Time Life Pictures/Getty Images

120-121: Image courtesy of The Neon Museum, Inc. Copyright held by The Neon Museum, Inc.

123: Tommy "Moe" Raft; From Harold Minksy Collection / UNLV Special Collections

124: *Crazy Horse* at the MGM Grand
Courtesy of MGM MIRAGE

128: Frank Costello, half-length portrait, seated, behind microphone, testifying before the Kefauver Committee investigating organized crime] / World Telegram & Sun photo by Al Aumuller, 1951
Miscellaneous Items in High Demand, Prints & Photographs Division, Library of Congress, LC-USZ62-120716

133: Moe Dalitz, Elvis Presley, Juliet Prowse, Wilbur and Toni Clark, Cecil Simmons, Joe Franks (standing behind W. Clark)
UNLV Special Collections

136: Wilbur Clark stands in front of Desert Inn
UNLV Special Collections

140: OCEAN'S ELEVEN, Frank Sinatra, Dean Martin, Sammy Davis Jr., Peter Lawford, Joey Bishop, 1960
Courtesy Everett Collection

142: Tremendous trio, 1961 January
Miscellaneous Items in High Demand, Prints & Photographs Division, Library of Congress, LC-DIG-ppmsca-24371

146: OCEAN'S ELEVEN, (aka OCEAN'S 11), Frank Sinatra, Patrice Wymore, 1960
Courtesy Everett Collection

150: Muhammad Ali standing over a fallen Sonny Liston in a boxing ring, 1965
Miscellaneous Items in High Demand, Prints & Photographs Division, Library of Congress, LC-USZ62-120902

152: Boxing match: Corbett - Fitzsimmons fight, 1897 March 17
Bain Collection, Prints & Photographs Division, Library of Congress, LC-USZ62-59410

160: HELL'S ANGELS, producer and director Howard Hughes, on location, ca. 1928-30
Courtesy Everett Collection

166: Liberace, ca. early 1970s
Courtesy Everett Collections

170: WHEN THE BOYS MEET THE GIRLS, Liberace, 1965
Courtesy Everett Collection

174: VIVA LAS VEGAS, Elvis Presley, 1964
Courtesy Everett Collection

178: ELVIS ON TOUR, Elvis Presley, James Burton on guitar, 1972
Courtesy Everett Collection

182: SIEGFRIED AND ROY, 1994, with one of their rare, Royal White Tigers.
Courtesy Everett Collection

186: Secret Garden - White Tiger
Courtesy of MGM MIRAGE

191: 21, (aka TWENTY ONE), Liza Lapira, Kate Bosworth, 2008. ©Columbia Pictures/Courtesy Everett Collection

195: The Wynn Las Vegas and Encore
iStock Photo

199 top: Front entrance to Dunes Hotel, Las Vegas, c. 1950s.
Credit: Union Pacific Railroad/UNLV Special Collections

199 bottom: The Bellagio
Courtesy of MGM MIRAGE

202: Fremont Street Experience
Las Vegas News Bureau

204: CityCenter with Crystals
Courtesy MGM Resorts International

210: Roulette
Las Vegas News Bureau

213: Scenes of open gambling in Reno, Nevada casinos: "overland roulette game, 1910 Oct 8
Miscellaneous Items in High Demand, Prints & Photographs Division, Library of Congress, LC-USZ62-64632

215: Scenes of open gambling in Reno, Nevada casinos: game of faro; many spectators, 1910 Oct. 8
Miscellaneous Items in High Demand, Prints & Photographs Division, Library of Congress, LC-USZ62-64635

220: Slot machines at a casino in Las Vegas, Nevada.
Courtesy: CSU Archives / Everett Collection

223: Slot Machine
iStock Photo

226: Glitter Girl neon sign at the Freemont Street Experience, Las Vegas, Nevada
Highsmith (Carol M.) Archive, Prints & Photographs Division, Library of Congress, LC-DIG-highsm- 04650

228-229: The Las Vegas Strip
Courtesy of Las Vegas News Bureau

240: Garth Charlton, 9th & Olive Photography
9olive.net

ACKNOWLEDGEMENTS

Museyon Guides would like to thank the following individuals and organizations for their guidance and assistance in creating *Chronicles of Old Las Vegas*:

Jessica Kaye
Las Vegas Convention and Visitors Authority
The Library of Congress Prints and Photographs Division
Los Angeles Public Library
MGM Resorts International

MGM Mirage
National Nuclear Security Administration / Nevada Site Office
Neon Museum
Patricia Scarpace
Springs Preserve
UNLV Special Collections

ABOUT MUSEYON

Named after the Museion, the ancient Egyptian institute dedicated to the muses, Museyon Guides is an independent publisher that explores the world through the lens of cultural obsessions. Intended for frequent fliers and armchair travelers alike, our books are expert-curated and carefully researched, offering rich visuals, practical tips and quality information.

Pick one up and follow your interests...wherever they might go.

For more information vist www.museyon.com

Publisher: Akira Chiba
Editor-in-Chief: Heather Corcoran
Media Editor: Jennifer Kellas
Art Director: Ray Yuen

Cover Design: José Antonio Contreras
Maps & Illustration Design: EPI Design Network, Inc.
Copy Editor: Cotton Delo

JAMES ROMAN

After regaling readers with his *Chronicles of Old New York*, James Roman returns to Museyon Guides with more chronicles, this time from the American West.

As a writer based in Los Angeles, Mr. Roman has lectured at the University of Southern California, served as Editorial Contributor to *New York Living* magazine for six years, and contributes regularly to publications that document emerging technology.

In Las Vegas casinos, he is notoriously lucky at Roulette.

Discover one of America's most fascinating cities on a tour through the glamorous and sometimes sordid history of Las Vegas. Find out how a railroad town transformed itself into "The Entertainment Capital of the World." Explore the major historic events from the founding of "Sin City" to the building of the Hoover Dam, from the rise of the Rat Pack at the Sands to Bugsy Siegel's Flamingo and the establishment of the Mafia-controlled casinos. Experience more than 150 years of history as you walk in the footsteps of Elvis, Liberace and Siegfried and Roy.

> 30 dramatic true stories

> 28 detailed maps

> 60 period photographs and illustrations

US $18.95

Cover Design: José A. Contreras

ISBN 978-0-9846334-1-8

51895 >

EAN

9 780984 633418